Sustainability in action in Britain?

Gillian Symons

WWF

© WWF-UK (World Wide Fund For Nature), 1997
Registered Charity No. 201707.

Published by WWF-UK, Panda House, Weyside Park,
Godalming, Surrey GU7 1XR.

A catalogue record of this book is available from The
Briitsh Library.

Designed by Schermuly Design Co., London
Printed by Arrowhead Printing Ltd, Bordon
on recycled paper.

Contents

PART 1: *Introduction*

What is sustainable development?   5
How do we know if we've achieved it?   8
What is this book about?   11

PART 2: *The Case Studies*

The structure of the case studies   13
The Diggers and SeaSaw   14
West Wiltshire Local Exchange Trading System   25
Larchfield Community   35
Anglian Woodland Project   47
City Lands Redevelopment   61
● An overview   61
● The neighbourhood colleges   70
Synopses of the case studies   76

PART 3: *Follow up*

Key questions about the transition to sustainability   83
More thoughts on sustainability   84
Ways to use the case studies with groups   86
● Activity 1   86
● Activity 2   87
● Activity 3   88
● Activity 4   88
● Activity 5   89
● Activity 6   93

Addresses for further information   **93**

Acknowledgements   **94**

© Walter Segal Self Build Trust

PART 1

Introduction

What is sustainable development?

Concerned by signs that human lifestyles are damaging the environment, world leaders gathered together in June 1992 to formulate an action plan for the 21st Century. Agenda 21 was adopted by 179 heads of state at the United Nations Conference on Environment and Development (the Earth Summit) in Rio de Janeiro. Its stated intention was to "launch a global partnership for sustainable development" (Boutros Boutros-Ghali, Secretary-General, United Nations). It contains recommendations for a Local Agenda 21 to be agreed by each local authority around the world in "dialogue with its citizens, local organisations and private enterprises". Since then, sustainable development has become the new catch-phrase, used by governments, businesses and environmental pressure groups.

But what would a world that was developing sustainably look like? How would we make the transition? Is it happening already? How would it affect the little corner of the town, city, village or countryside that each of us lives in? Would we enjoy living in this sustainable world? And can it be achieved without radically restructuring the way industrial societies are organised?

Everyone seems to agree that we need sustainable development, but there is no clear consensus as to exactly what it means or how the transition can take place. According to Jonathan Porritt, there are currently about 65 definitions in circulation. Opinions range

Some viewpoints on development:

"Sustainable development is development that meets the needs of the present without compromising the ability of future generations to meet their own needs"
(World Commission on Environment and Development, 1987)

"The future of our children depends on our ability to learn to live in harmony with nature and each other. Sustainable development means that we cannot satisfy our own needs at the expense of those of future generations."
(Gro Harlem Brundtland, 1991, Save the Earth, ed. Jonathon Porrit)

"Industrial civilization is on a collision course with the environmental system that supports life as we know it."
(Al Gore,1991, Save the Earth)

"Every human society attempts to get organised within its own house. Each house rests on four pillars: the number of people, the level of available natural resources, environmental quality, and the intensity of economic development. If some pillars rise disproportionately (be it the number of inhabitants in poor countries or material consumption of goods in rich countries) the house becomes unbalanced. Today the whole planet is our common house and it is high time to get it back in balance."
(Michael Batisse, former Assistant Director General (Sciences) of UNESCO,1991, Save the Earth)

"A sustainable community lives in harmony with its local environment and does not cause damage to distant environments or other communities - now, or in the future. Quality of life and the interests of future generations are valued above immediate material consumption and economic growth."
(The Sustainability Indicators Research Project, 1994, The Local Government Management Board)

Sustainable development is development which "improves people's quality of life within the carrying capacity of the Earth's life support systems."
(Caring For The Earth, The Second World Conservation Strategy, 1991)

"The basic needs of all humanity – for food, clothing, shelter and jobs – must be met. This involves, first of all, paying attention to the largely unmet needs of the world's poor, which should be given overriding priority."
(World Commission on Environment and Development, 1987)

"The limits to development are not absolute but are imposed by present states of technology and social organisation and by their impacts upon environmental resources and upon the biosphere's ability to absorb the effect of human activities. But technology and social organisation can both be managed and improved to make way for a new era of economic growth."
(World Commission on Environment and Development, 1987)

"Governments... should support a community-driven approach to sustainability [that would] establish new community-based mechanisms and strengthen existing mechanisms to enable communities to gain sustained access to resources needed by the poor to overcome their poverty."
(Agenda 21, 1992)

"Sustainable development is not just another name for environmental protection. It is concerned with issues which are long term and effects which are irreversible. A new approach to policy making is required which does not trade off short term costs and benefits but regards some aspects of the environment as absolute constraints."
(UK Government Declaration on Sustainable Development, 1993)

broadly from those who believe that we must develop better technology to clean up the mess we are making and that economic growth is the only way to finance this, to those who believe that current human systems, driven principally by economics, are fundamentally unsustainable. Those holding the latter opinion suggest that nothing short of a complete rethink of the way we live and our relationship to nature will prevent us from ultimately destroying the very things we need for the survival of our species.

How do we know if we've achieved it?

Among the various definitions of sustainable development, two key assumptions reappear. These are:

● that entitlement to quality of life should be universal
● that in attempting to achieve this, it is not acceptable to damage the Earth's resources beyond their capacity to recover, as that would reduce the quality of life of future generations.

In industrialised societies, improving quality of life has usually been taken to mean 'more is better'. We are frequently told that an increase in consumer confidence, and therefore in spending and consumption, is the way to get people back to work (so that they can earn the money to improve their standard of living, which is equated with quality of life). Yet this depends on marketing methods that decrease our satisfaction with what we have in order to encourage us to buy more, with a consequent increase in resource consumption and waste production. This is both unsustainable and has little bearing on quality of life.

Internationally, politicians from both right and left judge success in terms of increased Gross National Product (GNP), which measures a country's money flows. Yet an acknowledged 'disaster' like the *Exxon Valdez* oil spill increased GNP by increasing the flow of money through insurance and compensation payments, the costs of civil and legal proceedings, and the cost of the clean up operation. At the same time, it damaged the Earth's natural resources and surely did not improve quality of life.

GNP increases when money is spent treating illness but cannot record those staying well. It places no value on unpaid work, so that a country is perceived as successful if its people spend more time earning money and pay others to do things which would traditionally have been done voluntarily, such as household maintenance, caring for children and the elderly, and growing and preparing food. It does, however, give value to damage limitation expenditure on such things as policing, security, insurance and pollution control, which cannot alone provide clean air or safe streets.

The New Economics Foundation (NEF) has developed a different set of measurements, the Indicator of Social and Economic Welfare (ISEW), which they suggest may be a more accurate indicator of quality of life. It includes measurements of health, security and environmental quality as well as economic factors, and subtracts spending to offset social and environmental costs. Interestingly, this measurement suggests that in Britain, while GNP and ISEW increased in tandem until the middle '70s, since then, although GNP has continued to rise, quality of life has begun to fall. This was echoed by findings in other economically developed countries.

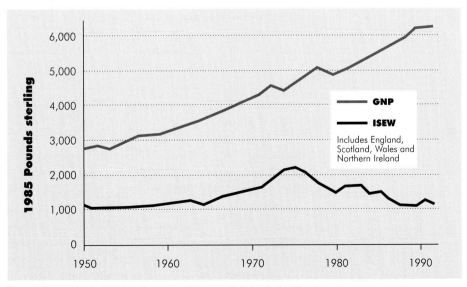

Source: Jackson and Marks, 1994, from Environmental Measures – Indicators for the UK environment

The NEF suggests that patterns of economic growth during the period since the 1970s have actually been the cause of the decline in sustainable economic welfare. This is because the rising toll of social and environmental costs, which are not measured by GNP, are beginning to have their effect in terms of welfare. The major factors, the NEF suggests, are the growing impact of resource depletion and long-term environmental damage, and the sharp increase in income inequality since 1974.

Ken Webster (*Reaching Out, Kirklees: Ideas for the Classroom*, 1994, WWF) suggests that the following set of criteria, may be used as indicators to measure the move towards sustainability, although he stresses that they are broad indicators which may not hold in every instance. They are less quantifiable than the ISEW, but are easier for the layperson to use.

1 The degree to which resource use is linear or cyclical

Are materials or energy being used so that waste is minimised by reuse, recycling or the use of renewable sources?

2 The degree to which human interaction is fragmentary or convivial

Do people meet in the course of their daily lives in a way which encourages them to undertake joint tasks or offer mutual support?

3 The extent to which production and consumption are international, national or local

Are the goods and services people use coming from within their own resources or local area? If so, the need for energy, materials, packaging and transportation will tend to be decreased. (Webster points out that this does not apply to information technology – telephone, video, electronics, etc.)

4 The degree to which the control of an activity is outside the control of local people or is exercised democratically by them

The more people control or influence the production of energy, goods and services, the more they are likely to be able to minimise pollution and environmental damage and ensure equitable costs and rewards. (Agenda 21 emphasises the need to involve hitherto disadvantaged groups, including the poor, women and young people, in the decision making process.)

5 The extent to which an activity diminishes the ecological base or promotes biodiversity

The more an activity reduces or simplifies a habitat, eg through monoculture or by certain fishing techniques, the more likely it is that biodiversity will be decreased. If it adds to the variety of the habitat, biodiversity will increase. Webster suggests that activities which fulfil the first four criteria will tend also to promote biodiversity.

What is this book about?

I set out to find the kind of things that groups of people in Britain are doing that "...improves people's quality of life within the carrying capacity of the Earth's life support systems" (*Caring for the Earth*, 1991), bearing in mind the criteria in the previous section, and the need for development to be ultimately economically, as well as socially and ecologically, sustainable.

I asked all sorts of people where I could go to see examples of sustainable development in action. People told me of wonderful grass roots projects in developing countries – but I wanted to find out what was possible here in Britain. People told me of remote, rural communities living sustainably with and from the Earth – but would they be seen as relevant to the majority of the population on our overcrowded island, who live in towns and cities? People told me that since Rio, many communities were trying to work out indicators by which they could measure whether they were living in more or less sustainable ways. But nobody I spoke to said, "This group of people in Britain are living sustainably, in a way that may be replicable on a larger scale". That was when the question mark crept into the title of this book.

I wanted to find ways of living that could not be dismissed as only for the few who can live outside the system. I questioned whether there is time for us to wait for all the small, grass-roots movements to change the direction of progress and, on the other hand, whether large scale initiatives, backed up by legislation and major financial inputs, are ultimately sustainable. Therefore, I wanted to look at projects on a variety of scales, to see if they could shed any light on this.

Finally, I made an almost random selection of projects that are happening in every day life in rural and urban communities. Through them, I hoped to explore some of the issues and processes involved in sustainable development and the barriers to its full achievement, ranging from personal attitudes to social systems. Many readers will know of similar or better examples.

I spent time with people involved with the projects and they told me their stories. In limited time, it was impossible for me to make accurate judgements about their long term commitments and lifestyles so, as far as possible, I have tried to allow the people involved to speak for themselves. Some of the people I talked to had never heard of sustainable development. Few of the projects fulfil all the criteria, but I feel that all of them have something to tell us about the processes leading to more sustainable ways of living and to a higher quality of life.

In the final section of the book, I have posed key questions and suggested activities through which I hope readers may draw their own conclusions about the processes involved with sustainable development.

PART 2

The Case Studies

The structure of the case studies

Each case study has been divided into five sections:

How did it come about?

This section explores the processes that groups went through in order for the project to happen and that individuals went through in order to become involved.

How does it help the environment?

This section looks at the environmental improvements created by the projects and the environmental impacts of the methods and resources used.

How does it affect the people involved?

Here, I wanted to explore the impact, if any, on the quality of life and personal attitudes of the people participating.

Has participation increased involvement with broader issues?

As I am interested in working towards a sustainable global community, I thought it important to find out if involvement in local initiatives had broader ramifications. Did people make connections between what was happening to them and wider issues?

...And the downside?

I wanted to explore whether the projects were sustainable in themselves, whether they were replicable by other groups and in other areas, and what the barriers were to their success. I am grateful that everyone I spoke to was honest about the difficulties, both personal and institutional, that they faced and believe that anyone wishing to work towards sustainability can learn as much from their perceptions of the problems as they can from their successes.

The Diggers and SeaSaw

Walter Segal was an architect who believed in the "sheer wealth of talent of ordinary people". Ample justification for this belief can be found in Brighton at The Diggers, where five families and four single people are living in light, spacious houses that they have built themselves and at SeaSaw, where 24 mainly unemployed people are working together as their houses take shape on a sloping site overlooking the sea.

How did it happen?

Gabrielle Sanders made the decision to get involved in self build after a visit to a mortgage broker to enquire about a mortgage for a two bedroom house for herself and her daughter, Christina. As a teacher, she had thought she would be in a reasonable position to buy, but the broker told her he couldn't begin to lend her enough. He offered her two possibilities if she wanted to be rehoused: either she abandon her career and go on the dole, or make plans to be married. Previously, she had wondered if she had the time or energy for self build, but given these options she decided, as she put it, "to build the classiest council house I've ever seen".

Steve Cole, the SeaSaw treasurer, who got involved through a friend, saw it as an opportunity to learn carpentry skills, to have secure housing and to be in charge of his own environment. Tommy Slattery, also of SeaSaw, was unemployed and living in poor quality rented accommodation when he saw an advertisement in the local paper asking for people who were interested in building their own home. Like others who responded, Tommy had to prove that he was in housing need. The majority of people on the scheme were unemployed and either on the Council waiting list for housing or suffering from "horrible landlord syndrome" (Steve). Alison confirmed this as she pumped insulation into the walls of a neighbour's house, telling a story of four landlords in six years, two of whom had tried to get her out.

Providing for their own housing needs was possible for people with no previous building skills, because of the Segal approach. Walter Segal had realised that timber frame houses with walls built from materials that can be bought from any builders merchants and assembled on site, involving no brick laying or plastering, would be simple enough for anyone to build. The Walter Segal Self Build Trust has been set up to continue his work and to offer information, advice, support and training to people, especially those on low incomes and in housing need, to build decent homes for themselves. As Mike Daligan, director of the Trust, explained, self build is traditionally the way most people are housed throughout the world, but "the concept of people building their own homes is an art that has become lost to the majority of the people of these islands mainly, I suspect, because most people simply do not believe that it is possible for them to do so."

Having taken up the challenge, Gabrielle and neighbours from the housing co-operative where she was living in overcrowded conditions, formed a new co-op and got talking to the people they would have to convince in order to get the money and the land they needed. After several years of negotiation, during which they advertised through the Council housing list, community groups and notices in local shops for additional members, they finally persuaded the Borough Council to give them the steeply sloping, derelict site of a disused golf club on the outskirts of Brighton. They also secured a grant from the South London Family Housing Association, from whom they will rent the houses at a cost around 70% of the level appropriate for the size of the properties, in recognition of the saving in labour costs to the association.

SeaSaw were slightly more fortunate in that they were supported by the Council from the beginning, but it still took them years to to get on site. 80% of their costs are also covered by a Housing Association grant.

How does it help the environment?

Being light weight and on a timber frame above the ground, the houses need only small 'pad' foundations, so they can be built on sites too sloping for traditional buildings, among mature trees, without disturbing the land. The buildings can be designed around the landscape rather than being imposed upon it. In consequence, there are still "lizards and frogs crawling about all over the site" at The Diggers. Money for planting was costed into the SeaSaw scheme and some of the group are getting advice about appropriate Downland plants. They are keen to plant some of the rarer wild flowers to contribute to the ecology of the area.

Wildlife at The Diggers is encouraged further by the turf rooves, which were also welcomed by the planners who were concerned about the high density of building in the area. The turf is a Sussex Downland mix full of wild flowers, which withstands drought and provides a habitat for local wildlife. It changes with the seasons. Gabrielle told me, "In May the rooves look wonderful, they're green and lush and all the flowers come out. By June, it's all dry and looks like a thatch and it blows around like a cornfield. In November it gets all beaten around by the wind. The designs are aesthetic as well as just functional."

She had an amusing story about self builders and wildlife learning to share the same habitat. When she first moved in after the building had been closed up for a while, there were two piles of about 200 dead bees by the windows, where they had been getting in through ventilation holes. She swept them up and the next day there were two more piles, but they were much smaller. The following day there were only four dead bees and now they still nest in the roof but never come into the house. As Gabrielle put it, "Some of them must have gone back and done a dance of warning, or something".

The frames of the houses at both sites are made from soft wood from sustainable sources. At SeaSaw, some of the builders have bought kitchens from a local contact who uses recycled wood. Stains and emulsions are organic and non-toxic. The walls are insulated with Warmcell which is made from recycled newsprint. Warmcell does not need the vapour control barriers required by most insulation and the resultant 'breathing walls', which let water vapour through, are much healthier to live in than the 'plastic bag' effect of traditional insulation.

The design of the houses makes the most of passive solar heating with a south-facing conservatory as a buffer to the living areas, roof lights, and smaller windows on the North side. All this, combined with double glazing throughout, makes them some of the best-insulated houses in the country. Additional heating is provided by high efficiency, condensing boilers. Instead of being turned on automatically by a time switch, this system calculates heat loss and turns itself on at an appropriate time to maintain required temperatures at different times of day, avoiding the usual problems of heating levels being inappropriate when outside temperatures change. This system is reckoned to be 85% efficient as compared to the 70% efficiency of a normal boiler and, combined with insulation and passive solar gain, means that heating costs are about £50 a year for a 3 bedroom house.

Mike considers self build to make a variety of contributions to the area in which it is situated. He talked of the environmental advantages of a system that can use derelict sites, telling a story of a person living in a house overlooking a self build, who thanked the builders for increasing the value of his house by giving him a view of trees and birds (and houses!) from his window, where previously there had been a dump. Self build also provides stable communities, as people rarely want to move on from a home they have designed and built themselves, particularly as the houses are so easily added to or adapted to suit changing family circumstances.

How does it affect the people involved?

Building their own houses involves a high degree of co-operation between the builders. They must work together, sometimes for years, to secure funding and land. They must develop teams to work on each building in turn – no one person could erect a 30 foot frame alone. As the builders often have other jobs or childcare responsibilities, timing needs to be co-ordinated so that there is always someone there to receive deliveries. Even after they have moved in at The Diggers, the communal garden is awaiting attention and the outside lighting needs to be installed.

This has its down side, demanding high levels of tolerance. Gabrielle talked of a day when she and one other person had to carry in all the bathroom units because no-one else was there. People borrow tools and lose them. There have to be a lot of group meetings at every stage. But Gabrielle knows that she would have been unable to do it on her own. She talks about the high level of understanding among the group, a result of being forced to work together through the difficult times. She says she never has to worry about emergency child care, or being afraid, or running out of something. She always has friends around her. Alison echoed this, saying she has never known so many neighbours. In her old home, she didn't even know the people living on either side.

Steve talked of the range of people he is building with, aged from 20s to 60s, many of whom he would never have met in other circumstances. They have separate gardens, without a lot of shared land, unlike The Diggers, but will still have to co-operate after they have moved in, becoming a co-op to manage the estate. They will have access to the maintenance fund and by doing the work themselves they can keep the rents down. As Steve said, "Who better to maintain a building than the people who built it?"

On a personal level, all the self builders talk about the increased confidence it has given them, so that they now feel that they can do anything they set their minds to. As Tommy put it, "It's great to have your own home, build it yourself, it's reallly marvellous. And the skills you learn… It keeps you active when work is scarce and you have something to show at the end of it."

Gabrielle talked of the effects on Christina of having seen her mother build her own house, saying "Her expectations of what it is possible for a woman to do will be so vastly increased. She'll consider that she is capable of doing almost anything that she decides to do." She said that friends who had seen what she had achieved had "kicked themselves into a different gear about what is possible for them". She quoted someone she had met on a self build in Newcastle, whose wife had been a drug addict and who was now looking after his three children on his own and building a house. He told her that self build isn't about building a house, it's about building yourself. Several people emphasised the special importance of self build for disenfranchised young people who are given skills, a real role and a sense of achievement. Mike Daligan linked the confidence and increased motivation gained by self builders with their increased ability to go out and look for work.

At SeaSaw, only five or six people came with building skills, but several of the others are now hoping to set up in self employment using their new skills. However, there was some disappointment that the building experience they have had will not receive recognised qualifications as it has on other schemes, due to their particular site manager being opposed to training, feeling it took time from the building work itself. As well as building skills, the group who volunteered to be responsible for most of the negotiations with the Council and the Housing Association have learned negotiating skills and how to read documents and legal information.

Alison felt that her participation in meetings had made her more able to speak up in front of a large group of people. She also felt she had learned through the team work. It is possible to get left out with such a large group and to be unsure of what to do, which she had found scary at first, but she had learned not to be afraid to ask and had discovered that to get there early each day ensured that she was part of a team.

Fourteen people on the site are doing employment training in horticulture, which was arranged by one of the members, using the build as their placement. Gabrielle had an unusual employment opportunity when she was selected to present a Channel 4 programme on self build as part of the *Gimme Shelter* season, and this has lead to further presenting work. Builders from earlier schemes are now using their experience to become contract managers for new schemes.

On top of all this, the self builders have created high quality environments for themselves. As Steve put it, "We've got an emotional input into this because we're going to live here and be stuck with what we've built. If you're working on your own house or your friend's house, that you've been working with for 18 months, you're not going to do a slap job on it."

Has participation raised involvement with broader issues?

 Gabriel emphasised the value of living in an environmentally friendly building and experiencing the benefits first hand, and feels it has put the long term benefits – "spend now to save for the future" – in the forefront of her mind. She has been asked to join a group promoting positive technology and thinks there has been an increase in awareness in most people on the site. Although many of them were already quite environmentally aware, their own achievements have made them realise what is possible. The knowledge of their own power to change their situation makes them more inclined to take action over the things that concern them.

Steve has become so interested in environmental issues through his involvement with SeaSaw that he has bought a book on ecology for beginners. As he says, we are all the end users of resources and when he sees programmes about deforestation in Brazil, he has the satisfaction of knowing his home is built from wood from a managed source. With his increasing knowledge, he finds himself talking to friends about the issues. The project has caused interest locally and has been visited by two groups of local primary school children who have used it as a basis for work about conservation.

Involvement in the negotiating team has made Steve much more politically aware. He used to think that people who demonstrated were either stroppy or doing it for a laugh, but having seen a number of high level people from the Housing Association move on to promotion in other organisations, after making decisions that will affect his life, he is now more aware of the need to stand up for his own rights and needs. Mike pointed out the risks of having a lot of people with increased confidence, skills and awareness, wanting to have their say in how things should be run, but felt in the long run, it would be far better for the country than the system we have now.

Gerard, another builder, thought that for most people their involvement with SeaSaw was a step on the gradual evolution of their thinking but was not going to change their basic position. While some people chose to get involved with negotiations and decision making on behalf of the group and were concerned about the environmental implications, there were others who just wanted a house and wanted as little as possible to do with the other aspects. However Alison, who has always had environmental interests, believes, "We can work on those people now we are living so close." She thought that awareness raising would take time but that people were already showing signs of change in their ability to work together. She said, "I think we're maturing as a group." She considered the range of opinions in the group, both politically and in lifestyle, to be healthy.

The Walter Segal Self Build Trust are thinking laterally in their quest to promote self build more widely. They have had links with the Centre For Alternative Technology since the early days, running courses there and producing joint publications. They are considering whether credit unions could become a part of the funding mechanism, and a trustee has recently suggested that they should be looking at where the Segal method fits in with Agenda 21, using this as a lever to encourage local Councils to provide land for self build.

And the down side?

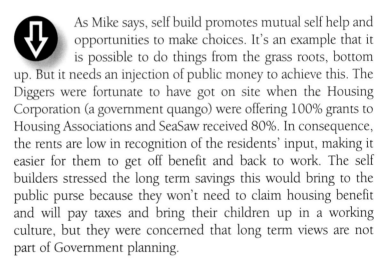

As Mike says, self build promotes mutual self help and opportunities to make choices. It's an example that it is possible to do things from the grass roots, bottom up. But it needs an injection of public money to achieve this. The Diggers were fortunate to have got on site when the Housing Corporation (a government quango) were offering 100% grants to Housing Associations and SeaSaw received 80%. In consequence, the rents are low in recognition of the residents' input, making it easier for them to get off benefit and back to work. The self builders stressed the long term savings this would bring to the public purse because they won't need to claim housing benefit and will pay taxes and bring their children up in a working culture, but they were concerned that long term views are not part of Government planning.

This has been borne out by a 1988 Treasury decision to slash public funding to Housing Associations from an average of 75% to an average of 58%, the rest of the money having to be borrowed from private sources. This inevitably means higher rents and as well as limiting residents' prospects of finding work, could affect motivation. As Gabrielle said, "Why should people take two years out of their lives to build houses for the Council when they're not going to get any reduction in recognition of their input?" Members are already disappointed that under current funding regulations they will never be able to own the homes they have built. (*It has since been announced that a new law will extend the right to buy to Housing Association tenants.)

There is also concern that the need for private finance may limit the design options, such as turf rooves. As Steve put it, "If you are trying to get a fund together when you're on the dole with no skills, putting forward plans that aren't conventional, it can be very difficult. The system just isn't geared to different things."

On a more personal level, the builders often have to put the rest of their life on hold in order to complete the building. At SeaSaw, everyone was contracted to put in 24 hours per week, but this was increased to 30 hours for 8 months as they had slipped behind schedule due to bad weather which made it difficult for those in or seeking work. Gabrielle found the combination of part time teaching, building and looking after a young child impossible to maintain, and with child care support stretched beyond the limit, she resigned from her job a term into the project.

Steve is concerned that the tightening of regulations regarding eligibility for social housing will exacerbate this situation. As someone who would have been unable to raise a private mortgage, through this scheme he has been able to build a home. The skills he has learned, combined with a reduced rent will, he hopes, enable him to set up as a self-employed carpenter. He would like to have a family in the future and in his current situation, he is very hopeful that he will be able to provide for them. However, as a single person, he would no longer fulfil the criteria for funding under social housing provision which is usually only available to people with children. He pointed out the impracticallity of spending two years building a house when you have young children to look after, but that the system is not geared to supporting young people to build their own homes before they have children.

There sometimes seems to be a problem with the 'professionals' involved genuinely wanting to give control to the builders. The architects, site managers and Housing Association workers have the technical skills but not all of them have the personal skills essential to implementing a full consultation process. One of the great things about self build is the amount of choice the builders have about the design of their own homes. But at a meeting at SeaSaw, site architects gave them ten minutes to decide what size windows they wanted. The energy implications were not explained and some people were more altruistic than others, thinking that if they asked for what they wanted, there might be less for others. The importance of giving time to the consultation and group decision making processes is not always understood by highly paid professionals for whom time is money. There was a feeling that the architects could have done more to educate the builders about the environmental aspects of the scheme and that although they would talk about this with enthusiasm to people they needed to impress, they hadn't bothered to use the opportunity with the builders themselves, who were a captive audience.

The Housing Association wanted to treat the self builders in the same way as their other tenants, with, the group felt, little recognition of their enormous physical and emotional input. It took two years of negotiation and 15 amendments to the original building contract before they felt sufficiently empowered within the decision making process. For example, the scheme at SeaSaw now has yearly rent increases linked to inflation and not to "the whims of Housing Association committees who raise rents on all properties in order to expand their size and influence" (Steve).

The Government Housing Minister was at the opening of The Diggers, talking of Government support for the scheme, while at the same time the Housing Association grants were being reduced. As Steve put it, the opening was all about "people in suits giving awards to other people in suits". One of the builders wanted to speak about problems that had arisen during the project and the way future self build schemes could be improved, but he wasn't allowed to "in case he rocked the boat".

There was a general feeling that the self builders had to fight all the way to maintain control over their schemes. The Walter Segal Trust is co-ordinating potential self builders, architects, local authorities and other landowners, building societies and other financial institutions but unless there is a genuine willingness to give real power to the builders themselves, the current blossoming of such hopeful schemes is likely to founder. However, as Mike put it, if societies don't spend money in positive ways, they have to spend it later on control.

West Wiltshire Local Exchange Trading System

Increasingly, the belief in economic growth as the route to human happiness is coming into question. There is growing awareness of the importance of other 'quality of life' factors, such as satisfying work, a sense of community, access to resources and services, and a sense of control over one's own life. The rapid expansion of Local Exchange Trading Systems (LETS) may be one symptom of this.

LETS work through a form of barter but with greater flexibility than the traditional one-to-one exchange. Members use a local directory to advertise their skills and products, and to locate others providing services they need. Work is paid for through a cheque book based on a local currency, which in Warminster is called Links. Personal accounts are debited and are balanced by providing goods or services for someone else.

How did it happen?

Liz Shepherd set up the West Wiltshire LETS, the first of its kind, in 1990. Her work with new economics, a sense that the banks and the money system itself are a driving force behind the environmental crisis, and experience through social work of the break down of communities, led her to look for community based initiatives that would tackle poverty. She wanted to develop a model that could be tested and that would be replicable in other countries.

She was drawn towards the idea of local currencies because her research had shown both recent and historic examples of local currencies transforming destitute local economies. Their main advantage is that they do not need an injection of external capital,

Green pounds reach the parts other currencies can't

which Liz considers an essential factor if systems are to be empowering and replicable. They start from where people are, in areas of need, as opposed to the ineffective 'trickle down' effect of top down approaches.

Local groups grow mainly through word of mouth, with founder members bringing in friends, business contacts and people from other groups with which they are involved. LETS have received considerable media interest so when people see posters about local schemes, they may link them with an article they have read and decide to find out more. Warminster LETS now has about 450 members.

Liz explained that trading without 'real' money demands changes in people's habits and may be slow to begin. Once a new register is set up, there is usually a lull while everyone waits for everyone else to call. After a slow start, trading suddenly increases dramatically as stories of successful exchanges spread and understanding grows of how to make best use of the scheme. In Warminster, three years of steady growth in members were followed by a six month period with a leap in turnover greater than the preceeding three years put together.

LETS members Trace Senior and Harry Turner had both originally been sceptical about the idea and had finally been forced into involvement because personal misfortune, a broken neck in one case and mental breakdown in the other, removed other options. Some people join to keep a flagging business viable, others out of a desire to put something back into the community in which they live.

Liz sees LETS as an idea whose time has come. In 1985, when she began researching local currencies, it had limited appeal; but the recession, with increased unemployment and a lack of obvious solutions, has lead to increased interest in alternative approaches.

The responsibility of local Councils to implement Local Agenda 21 has encourged some Councils to adopt LETS as part of their strategy of sustainable development, and some are even funding LETS development workers. Liz believes that the benefits LETS provide by meeting needs as they arise instead of waiting till they reach crisis proportions improves human environments, saves money from public coffers and should be of interest to any government.

How does it help the environment?

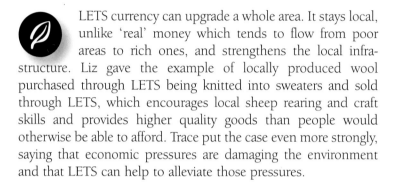

LETS currency can upgrade a whole area. It stays local, unlike 'real' money which tends to flow from poor areas to rich ones, and strengthens the local infrastructure. Liz gave the example of locally produced wool purchased through LETS being knitted into sweaters and sold through LETS, which encourages local sheep rearing and craft skills and provides higher quality goods than people would otherwise be able to afford. Trace put the case even more strongly, saying that economic pressures are damaging the environment and that LETS can help to alleviate those pressures.

LETS save resources. Unlike in the traditional economy, labour is cheaper than materials and non-human energy sources which often have to be purchased in hard currency from outside the trading area. Therefore people offer repair services. Goods and services are often of a higher quality and longer lasting, being hand made for people known to the maker. Resources such as tools and machinery are shared and exchanged, while the use of human energy is maximised.

Keynes suggested that exporting information, knowledge and culture while keeping the provision of goods as local as possible would provide a balanced economy. LETS encourage the local provision of goods and services. This reduces the need for transportation which in turn reduces pollution and associated health problems and the demand for road building, with its environmental implications. Local businesses can be enabled to survive through the existence of LETS networks and distribution systems so that people don't have to travel out of the area for work.

Liz believes the current economy to be devoted to throughput and short-term thinking, making it hard to get the long-term investment which is necessary for the future of people and of the environment. LETSLink are looking into the possibility of setting up pension schemes which will be funded by planting tree seeds which will be harvestable in 70 years time. LETS labour is accepted as matching funding for certain grants, and LETS networks can identify the hidden needs and human resources to develop sustainable projects that would otherwise not get off the ground.

How does it affect the people involved?

Trace, a married man with two young children, broke his neck in a car crash. When asked about the effect of LETS on his family, his response was, "After my accident, there were times when cash was so hard for us that we ran out of money and if it hadn't been for LETS, we wouldn't have eaten". His family paid in Links for freezer meals. These were provided by a local smallholder who uses LETS labour to help her grow food which she then harvests, prepares, freezes and delivers to other members.

The benefits of LETS are both social and economic. Liz says marriages have been kept together simply because access to babysitters has taken the pressure off unemployed families. She stressed the sense of place and community that LETS trading can provide to isolated individuals. Extended family patterns are created when an elderly babysitter becomes an honorary grandmother and in return can get help with gardening and odd jobs. People with mental health problems find peer group support as well as services such as counselling or acupuncture. 'Gift' relationships develop after a while as the need to record reciprocal transactions between two people falls away.

Small businesses such as painting and decorating and retailing can be kept afloat by accepting part payment in local currency. Potential new businesses are able to test consumer response through LETS trading, which provides them with a successful launch pad without having to incur a massive bank overdraft. People can receive training, either through skill sharing or tutoring in things as diverse as computer skills, cheese making and dressmaking. LETS traders train young people in basic skills such as door hanging and washing windows by taking them out on the job.

By providing instant, interest free credit for urgently needed goods and services, LETS can replace the need for money lenders for the 25% of the population without bank accounts and can help people to keep out of debt. Needs can be met as they arise instead of being left through lack of ready money until they reach crisis proportions. The sense of community can help to decrease crime and increase feelings of safety. Much disease is stress and pollution related and loss of morale, feelings of alienation and drink and drugs problems are often related to unemployment and economic difficulties which are alleviated by LETS.

LETS schemes include a wide mix of people from those out of full time employment to people running their own businesses and those in professional occupations, for all of whom the schemes have different benefits. Liz gave the example of a doctor who joined out of a sense of commitment to put something into his community, offering the loan of equipment because he had no time to offer services. He then found that through LETS he could get services which were not easily available on the open market such as house sitting and dog walking.

Another Warminster LETS member got involved through using the washing machine in a neighbour's house. To pay back his debts, he began working with the 'garden gang'. He became interested in starting his own business and got both business advice and desk top publicity through LETS.

Harry credits his involvement with LETS as a major factor in his recovery from mental health problems brought about by the breakdown of a 23 year marriage and separation from his children. On his birthday, unemployed and in the depths of depression, he had called the mental health services who offered him an appointment a week later. He was fortunate that his landlady suggested he might get immediate support through LETS, and within an hour he was visited by an acupuncturist and the road to recovery began. He repaid his LETS debt by giving lifts, was offered cups of tea on arrival, and rapidly found himself part of a supportive community.

As an ex-art teacher he then offered art classes through LETS which eventually led to an exhibition. At the exhibition one of his students, who also suffered from depression, sold a painting for LETS credits. This recognition for her work improved her self esteem and eventually lead to further exhibitions through which she earned 'real' currency.

Harry became increasingly convinced of the value of LETS for mental health. As well as providing for immediate needs without money worries, it cuts through the social isolation and stigma that often exacerbate mental illness, increasing feelings of self worth and facilitating friendships and a sense of community. He invited the local mental health group to a meeting of the Warminster LETS which lead to a ten week 'induction to LETS' programme at the mental health centre drop-in. Among other things, this helped people to identify skills they could offer. An initial lack of confidence among participants lead to the idea of initially trading only among themselves. A self help system was set up among the group which provided a crisis phone line and a cleaning and shopping service for members in times of particular need. As Harry put it, "The best tool to get yourself better is to help someone else to get better."

He explained that a common pattern in mental illness begins with people being given support by the official services in times of crisis. When they are better this is withdrawn and after a time they deteriorate again until another crisis brings renewed help. The self help structure provides constant support and social contact which breaks this cycle. As well as encouraging self help, the Warminster LETS has a dozen trained counsellors among its members. The local Health Service have been supportive of the scheme and have provided space at a local health centre for acupuncture, tai chi, art and music classes to be set up, all of which can be paid for with LETS currency.

This scheme has been so successful that after articles in the LETSLink magazine, Harry has had enquiries from 20 other mental health groups around the country. Some have paid expenses for him to talk to their local group about the mechanics of setting up a mental health LETS and other groups are now under way.

Trace can do little housework or gardening with his injury. He lost his company car and is unable to walk far. As well as getting help through LETS with basic jobs around the house, LETS lifts enabled him to collect the children from school. He paid his debts by sharing his computer skills. But the effects were far wider than mere practical support. He and his children have met a lot of people from different backgrounds and he is excited by the growing sense of community. He feels LETS helps to break down the class system.

He talked about the personal changes in attitude that being a member of a LETS had brought about in him. He was at first resistant to his wife's suggestion that they should join LETS, "Having been brought up in traditional business, I thought it was a lot of way out ideas and really not for me... If you're a professional person and you need things like food, there's this ego business – I think it's a male thing – mine got in the way for a long time. A lot of people think it's beneath them, it's an image thing. You've got to create an awareness whereby people realise it's about genuine changes in attitude towards trading. If a few people are willing to try and it's seen to be successful, the sceptics will get on board and it will snowball. It's a caring, sharing attitude that's really different in this day and age."

Has participation raised involvement with broader issues?

 LETS can draw together people with mutual needs but no common interest, therefore people hear viewpoints they would not normally be exposed to and there can be a cross fertilisation of ideas. Liz suggested that being given the resources to sort out their immediate problems provides people with space to take on wider issues. The participative, collaborative approach to providing for needs can change peceptions. She gave as an example the Japanese housewives who got together to buy cheap milk, whose group is now represented in local government due to their increased awareness of the power they had collectively to change things. This was reinforced by an observation made by Trace: "LETS helps people to understand that power is not about how much money you have, it's about growing together as a community, that's the way forward."

Trace felt his involvement with LETS had definitely increased his involvement in other local issues. "Getting involved with something like LETS gives you a lot more confidence to say I think this is wrong and I'm prepared to do something about it. I hate injustice but I never felt I could do anything about it; but now I think I can, and it's the support I've got from learning how to work with the LETS scenario that has allowed me to do that. Other people I've met who would never have said boo to a goose before are prepared to stand up and be counted. Ordinary people want a better world for their children and are starting to say we don't need outside help to change what we've got."

And the down side?

The feeling of unreserved optimism coming from the people involved in the Warminster LETS seems to be related to the great sense of empowerment they have through not being dependent on any outside source to provide money or resources to make the project work. As Trace expressed it, "It has to be led by local communities. It's non-sexist, non-racist, non-ableist – everyone can get involved."

The main concern was whether "the beaureaucracy of Government might knock it on the head" (Trace). Skill-swap schemes in the 1970s were stopped by the DSS and successful schemes on a large scale in Germany, Austria and the USA in the 1930s were stopped by the big banks. Currently LETS are accepted as long as people in business pay taxes on their LETS earnings as well as on sterling transactions. The appointment by some Councils of LETS development workers is a hopeful sign and Council support will help to spread the use of local currencies. Trace told the story of a tax office in Australia which decided to allow people to pay LETS taxes in kind because they needed their offices doing up. If Local Authorities accept part payment of rates in local currencies, it will become easier for shops and businesses to accept LETS currency as part payment.

The DSS response, however, needs positive clarification which may only be provided if and when systems are significantly larger in size. This uncertainty is currently deterring some unemployed people from becoming involved. The Australian DSS has just announced that it will fund LETS development, providing computers and training. However, there is a fear that governments may use LETS as an excuse for premature cuts in benefits. It remains to be seen whether the very success of LETS in reducing dependency on high interest loans in an economy where big profits are made through such practices, will bring about their downfall or whether they will be allowed to continue towards their goal of increased quality of life for all.

Larchfield Community

Larchfield is a community on the edge of Middlesborough, in which about 40 people, many with learning difficulties, live and work. Training and employment are also provided for non-residents. There is a farm, a market garden, a bakery, workshops for weaving and woodwork, and a cafe. Everyone, according to their ability, is expected to contribute towards the well being of the community. As far as possible, they live in harmony with the land, which is farmed according to biodynamic principles. All sewage is treated through a series of shallow ponds linked by reed beds which act as biological filters. Larchfield is one of many Camphill communities around the world which are inspired by the ideas of Rudolf Steiner.

© Iris Water
& Design

How did it come about?

Larchfield was set up in 1986 at the request of Middlesborough Council, after Council members visited another Camphill and decided that such a centre would fit well with the aims of the borough. The Council provided the land and put money into the conversion of existing farm buildings, opening the way to grant funding from a variety of other sources to establish the community. Now it runs on the social security payments for the residents with special needs, fees for providing training, and money earned from sales of farm produce and craft work. A stall in the weekly market provides an outlet for over half the community's market garden produce, the rest being consumed by the residents. Virtually all the farm produce is sold locally through conventional channels.

People have come to Larchfield through many different routes. Some people with learning difficulties have transferred from other Camphills to be nearer their families. Others have been referred by social services or heard about it through family or friends. Some co-workers became house parents because they thought it would be a good environment for their own children to grow up in. Others have come as temporary volunteers. Young people from Britain and abroad live and work there for a few months. Peter came for three years, and nearly nine years later is still there. Chris applied for a job as a baker through the local job centre and continued to live in his council house eight miles away. Now he and his wife Val and two children are staying at Larchfield, while they decide whether to make it their permanent home.

Workshop space and land is used by a market gardener, a baker, a joiner, caterers preparing freezer meals and business lunches, a vehicle mechanic and someone running a wild flower nursery. They are all non-residents who have free use of the facilities in exchange for providing training. This has evolved from the philosophy that everyone involved with Larchfield becomes a co-worker with a social responsibility to pass on their skills, whether to special needs residents, other co-workers or people on training courses. Everyone providing workshops is a member of a guild which helps with such things as health and safety requirements, insurance and setting up accredited courses.

Changing Government training schemes have brought in a wide range of trainees including long-term unemployed, school refusers, inmates from the local prison and people working for National Vocational Qualifications. Training takes place through working alongside skilled workers and greater responsibility is given to each person as they show themselves ready. This requires organisational flexibility and a readiness to accept change as individuals gain in confidence and skills or decline in strength.

A complex system of committees run the community. A management committee comprising Larchfield members and Councillors oversees its development. There is a weekly meeting to which everyone is welcome to come and share needs, wishes and problems. There is a land group, a finance group, a bakery group and a welfare and admissions group. A decision was taken that everyone should be involved with accounts, so although there is one main account, each area has its own accounts with different people responsible for them. A painting is to be bought for the hall and all the residents will help to choose one from an exhibition the community is organising as part of an art festival. Camphills have no voting system and decisions at any level are debated until there is consensus. It means a lot of meetings, but as Chris said, the proof of the pudding is in the eating. It works. The oldest adult Camphill community is about to celebrate its fortieth birthday and is still using the same system.

© *Iris Water*
& Design

The water treatment system for the whole community was designed by Iris Water and Design in consultation with residents. Everything that goes down the drains is fed into the first of three interlinking ponds, fringed with aquatic plants and linked to the others by reed beds. Water cascades through specially shaped 'flowforms' which maximise aeration. From the third pond, clean water runs into a drainage ditch and eventually into a lake in Middlesborough.

Biological sewage treatments have been in use for many years in different parts of the world. One third of sewage systems in the United States, around 1,000 systems in Germany, 2,000 in France and others in Scandinavia and Alaska incorporate stabilisation ponds. European systems serve up to 1,000 people each while systems in the US treat the effluent of up to 5,000 people and the city of Auckland has over 5 sq km of ponds. Experiments using natural and artificially created marshes to clean water began in the United States in the 1960s. The principle of the pond systems is that bacteria break down the sewage, producing carbon dioxide which feeds an algal population, which in turn provides the oxygen to keep the bacteria going. Iris have taken this further, concentrating on creating rich, varied wetland habitats to encourage a complete eco-system to develop, drawing energy up through a food pyramid, evidence of which was provided by the large families of mallards on the Larchfield ponds.

How does it help the environment?

The Camphill philosophy is to live in harmony with the natural world. They use an organic farming system called biodynamics which, Peter says, has given a scientific basis to instinctive, indigenous knowledge, recognising the interconnectedness of all aspects of life. They have created a range of habitats, including varied hedgerows. Larchfield is surrounded by 'shelter belts' of trees and shrubs which, according to Val, create a physical and symbolic break between organic and chemically treated land.

The water treatment system, as well as providing a rich habitat, is low in energy use. The only energy requirement is to pump the water into the 'flowforms', which reduce the land area needed, but Iris plan to use wind powered aerators on some systems in the future. Being completely biological, no chemicals are required for the treatment process and all residents are careful not to put damaging pollutants into the system. Future systems are looking at the possibility of recycling the cleansed water for agricultural irrigation or for toilet flushing, which would further increase the environmental benefits of the system.

Everything possible is recycled. Kitchen waste is composted, leaves are mulched and the community has a contract with a recycling company who collect their non-organic waste such as cans and bottles. The buildings were renovated according to the highest energy saving standards and every household has an Aga or Rayburn which uses solid fuel for the tripple purposes of cooking and space and water heating. Living in family groupings of up to twelve people reduces the energy used for cooking and heating and the need for resources such as washing machines and refrigerators. Vehicles are shared by the whole community.

The love and respect for everyone that characterises Larchfield extends to the treatment of the animals. Although animals are reared for meat, they are treated well and have plenty of space, out of doors as far as possible. Meat eating tends to be a weekly treat in many households rather than a daily necessity, because of the abundance of other tasty foods. The fox hunt is banned from Larchfield land, as residents consider tearing an animal apart while it is still alive to be unacceptable.

How does it affect the people involved?

 Chris arrived at the community wanting a job. He described himself as streetwise with a common sense approach and not really into environmental things. But when asked why he was now considering making Larchfield his permanent home, his unhesitating response was "love and affection – you don't get that from an ordinary job". The strong message was that everyone is on equal terms. Val explained that the Steiner approach is to look for what is inside a person and help it come out. There is a great sense of security that comes from a recognition of the validity of every individual's needs and abilities. Peter talked of a teenager who had dropped out of school after a breakdown and came to the community suffering from desperate insecurity and an inability to cope with other people. He moved on after four years, spent working first on the farm and then as an apprentice to the mechanic, with his confidence rebuilt and now has a full-time job in the town. The unthreatening nature of a community in which competition and comparisons between people have no place, but where the potential of every individual is recognised has a healing effect.

Peter explained, "We're about self reliance and interdependence, not self sufficiency." The philosophy is 'I sustain you with my work and you sustain me with yours'. Some enterprises make money, some don't, but they are all valued for their different contributions to the life of the community. For example, the bakery provides wholesome food, good training and brings in 'new' money from members of the public. It is not dependent on sales to pay wages, which are seen as the responsibility of the whole community.

There is a recognition that everyone's needs are different. This has its most concrete form in the allocation of money. For people who live at Larchfield, there are no 'wages'. Each household can use as much meat, fruit, vegetables, milk and eggs from the farm as it wishes and is given a weekly allocation from the central pot for additional food, household expenses and other needs. Co-workers do not have individual money, but household money can be drawn on for personal needs, and there is no guilt about using it to buy cigarettes or to pay for the occasional night out. Holidays are considered very important and everyone is encouraged to go away for at least three weeks, paid for from the common pot. Day workers are paid according to their own assessments of their needs. Chris and Val explained they worked out the cost of rent, food, bills, holidays, school uniforms, etc and asked for wages to cover this.

The recognition of individual needs extends beyond the immediate community. Val told a story of young people from the neighbouring estate driving around on motor bikes every night on an unused field. She said, "We thought they should be stopped, the police should be called, but people here said Why? They're not hurting anybody. There's a bit of noise, but it's keeping them out of more serious trouble. That's Camphill's attitude, they trust, they trust everybody, they always give you a second chance. They'll tell you if you do something wrong but then that's it, your second chance starts."

Peter said that people mature at Larchfield because everyone is expected to take responsibility. Val explained, "Nobody can make anybody work here but if people don't do their share, the whole place would fall apart. There would be no vegetables at the end of the year because they would have been strangled by the weeds; the animals would starve; if Jonathan didn't grease the bakery tins properly, the bread wouldn't be fit for sale. Everyone sees the consequences of their actions." For some of the residents who have learning difficulties and have previously lived in institutions, this can mean moving from agressive, institutionalised behaviour such as grabbing food, to a supportive awareness of the needs of others. For others who have previously lived with protective parents, it involves a recognition that they have an essential contribution to make.

Taking responsibility even extends to the water treatment system. As Chris Hudson from Iris said, most people have little idea of what happens to their sewage and waste water. As an 'environmentally aware' architect, Chris admitted that when drawing house plans previously, once he had drawn "that thin black line onto the mains" he hadn't thought further about what happened next. With pond and reedbed systems, everyone becomes aware of the implications of what they are putting down toilets and drains because the ponds are part of their immediate environment and, because the system is so simple, the users themselves are responsible for maintenance.

For some people, the close, ongoing relationship with the land has brought about the greatest changes. Peter said that when he arrived, he thought the three years he planned to stay was a long time and showed a lot of commitment. Now, after nine years, his commitment is growing. He says that traditionally farmers have generations of experience to call on and feels that after a long term commitment to one piece of land you get to know it and it begins to speak to you. He has a growing sense that every change displaces something elemental which needs to be harmonised again.

People talked a lot about the growing enjoyment gained from meaningful work, done for the pleasure of doing a job well, instead of because they're told to. Chris had been a baker all his life but he had never worked with organic ingredients before. It's much harder, because every bag of flour is different and demands different mixing, but he loves it. It doesn't get boring and he is proud of the skill it demands and its delicious taste.

Children enjoy growing up at Larchfield. They may get less personal attention from their parents, but are surrounded by people to play and work with. Richard is eleven and loves the freedom of Larchfield, with no worries about danger from vehicles or 'strange' people, which as Val says is ironic, because those with special needs are often considered strange in other environments.

An unexpected bonus of life at Larchfield for Chris has been a major improvement in his health. He's taken tablets almost every day for sixteen years since he developed arthritus at the age of 22. The only time he stopped, he nearly lost his eyesight. Since living at Larchfield, as well as loosing a stone in weight in a couple of weeks, he has stopped taking the tablets and is feeling great. Although he can't prove it, he's convinced it is due to eating organic food.

Has participation raised involvement with broader issues?

The lives of the Larchfield residents are mainly involved with their immediate community and environment. Peter felt the biggest change which would be of significance in the broader community was usually in the attitudes of trainees, day workers and visitors. They come thinking that people with special needs are 'wierd' but after working alongside them, their friendliness leads to a genuine acceptance and respect developing between the two groups, which will affect the trainees' perceptions of disabled people they meet in other situations.

Working on the land is considered low-status by most trainees, according to Peter, but he sited the example of one trainee who had developed a strong commitment to organic methods and had gone from Larchfield to train in horticulture as an example of a small number of long-term trainees whose outlook is changed by the experience.

Chris Hudson feels the water treatment system also affects people's perceptions – putting sewage in a pond being another aspect of Larchfield life that is considered 'wierd' by newcomers, but one that they grow to accept and understand. The concern to put water back into the environment in as clean a state as possible becomes important, alongside a growing awareness and avoidance of the factors which create water pollution. Planning permission for another system Iris were involved with had to be obtained from the Parish Council, who at first thought it would be a smelly health hazard but were converted once the real nature of the development was explained.

Peter stressed the growing recognition of process that comes from seeing what happens to your waste and from being involved with growing the food you eat and making choices about what goes into it. Val talked about the education that goes on in the cafe. For example, people comment on the delicious taste of the bread and workers can use this as an opportunity to explain how it is made and why they use organic ingredients. She said people begin to turn to organic food because their children become hyper-active or asthmatic on certain foods and find that this doesn't happen if it is organic. She and Chris tell of their own experiences of the benefits of eating organic food in the hope that it will influence other people.

And the downside?

A strong decision has been taken by the community to look carefully at the demands of different funders and to refuse money that may in any way affect the way they operate. This came from the experience of accepting Inner Area Programme money which had to be spent within a very short time and lead to the sudden expansion of the community at a pace with which they couldn't humanly cope. It made them realise that they were increasingly open to people coming from outside and dictating how they developed, and the decision was made that they had to look very carefully at the conditions attatched to funding in order to regain control.

They refuse to play what Peter describes as "the political game" of having to shape your work to fit the requirements of whoever has the biggest pot of money, which often depends on changing Government priorities. They find the whole notion of competing for funding which is then only available a year at a time works against their commitment to respond to differing needs. Training is an important part of their approach, but the Training and Enterprise Council's requirement for throughput works directly against the Larchfield belief that training must continue until a recipient feels confident to do the job. Peter says the TECs are now attempting to push people through training in six weeks, which he believes may give them a qualification but will not give them the experience and confidence to do a decent job.

He also talked about how the benefits system works against unemployed people who want to do an apprenticeship or volunteer work at Larchfield, but are unable to put in more than 16 hours a week without losing benefits. He feels the system works against people wanting to share their skills. He said that when the going gets tough the first thing to go is the apprenticeships, but difficult times are the very times when it is most important to think about the future.

Val and Chris see cost as a barrier for many people to the opportunity to eat the fresh, organic produce which has improved their health. They talked of the daughter of a relative whose asthma is badly affected by certain food additives, but whose parents cannot afford the additional cost of organic food. As they said, if you're on social security with five children, you buy the cheapest food. They feel that organic produce is expensive because of the larger labour force needed if chemical treatments aren't used. Current farming subsidies throughout Europe which reward farmers for neglecting set aside land as well as for high yields from the remaining land, work against the organic farmer and against employment opportunities in rural communities.

Various reports have suggested that there is no reason why biological water treatment systems should not be used more in Britain, particularly considering their widespread use in other countries. The main barrier seems to be the inertia that means things tend to be done the way they've always been done. Biological treatment requires land, therefore Chris Hudson considers it to be most suited to rural areas or on the edge of cities, where it can use derelict or marginal agricultural land, and less appropriate for crowded inner city areas. He stressed that waste stabilisation ponds are not a panacaea, but are a good environmental solution in appropriate situations.

Currently, only statutory water companies have access to Government and EC grants for sewage treatment systems. Chris feels that biological systems are unlikely to be built into new developments because connection to the mains costs the developer only a one-off charge, the running costs being returned to the householder via the water rates. Capital costs for natural water treatment would be higher and there would then be the question of who would be responsible for long-term management of the system. However, he is hopeful that as public awareness grows, the lower long term costs and environmental benefits may make decentralised treatment systems something that buyers are actually seeking, in the same way as buildings with high energy ratings are now easier to market.

Although Larchfield has a commitment to working with anyone who can benefit from being there, it is a relatively closed community, with different values from much of the world around it. Chris and Val are unsure how their children will cope with these conflicting values. As an example they talked about how Christmas at Larchfield, where people make presents for each other and 'small means a lot', would conflict with the competitive nature of Christmas among the children's school friends, for whom expensive mountain bikes and computer games were the norm. They wondered if a move to a Steiner school, which would share the values of Larchfield, may become necessary.

© Iris Water & Design

Anglian Woodland Project

Wood is a truly sustainable, renewable source of materials and energy. But forests in this country, as well as in the rest of the world, have suffered major decline as the land has been cleared for other uses and as bad management prevents natural regeneration. The Anglian Woodland Project was set up in 1991 to improve woodland management in small, neglected woodlands in the area and to stimulate new markets for woodland products. Its approach combines the importance of preserving and improving existing woodlands for their wildlife and conservation value with an awareness of the need to create jobs and provide an economic incentive for good management. In its area of operation, Bradfield Woods Nature Reserve provides an example of the potential of managed woodlands.

How did it happen?

The Forestry Commission joined together with the Countryside Commission and the County Councils of Cambridgeshire, Essex, Norfolk and Suffolk, to address the continued neglect of small woodlands in this part of the country. Bob Hands, the project director, describes it as a partnership to see what might be done for the future survival of this large resource. The initial aim was to raise awareness of the desirability of bringing the woodlands back into management, to dispel some of the myths that work against this (for example, that there are no markets for the produce of broadleaved woodlands) and to provide incentives and development programmes to help it to happen.

© Anglian
Woodland
Project

The area has many small, ancient woodlands of native broadleaf that have been in existence for hundreds of years. Clearances as a result of agricultural incentives to grow more food have lead to the existence of about 20,000 scattered woodlands all under different ownership, about 78% of which are not managed. Bob pointed out that without management, over time invasive species such as birch and sycamore will destroy the diversity of the sites which are important as a reserve sink for native species and eco-systems.

Bradfield Woods National Nature Reserve in Suffolk is a rare example of an ancient, coppiced woodland that has been managed in the same way for centuries. The first record of coppicing at Bradfield dates back to 1252 and until the middle of this century, the woods were recognised as a valuable asset, providing building materials, fencing, fuel and other wood products for the local area. Then with the introduction of agricultural grants in the 1960s, the owner began to sell off the woods. Recognising their value, local people mounted a major campaign and after four years the wood had a preservation order put on it but already a third of it had been cut down. Ironically, a third of the cleared land is again receiving agricultural subsidy, this time as set-aside. The woods are now managed by Suffolk Wildlife Trust with support from English Nature. Two full time staff, a part time education worker and a shifting population of volunteers maintain the woods, run an active education programme and market the produce.

Now the Anglian Woodland Project has its awareness raising programme well under way, the next phase is action planning, data collection and business creation. The project aims to hand over work created to the private sector but sees the role of the public sector as being to raise the profile, set standards and put systems into place. Bob says this is important in an area with little history of forest management, unlike in parts of the country where the infra-structure is already in place.

How does it help the environment?

Bob explained that all the project does is driven by the Helsinki and Rio biodiversity agreements, giving priority to the maintenance of a healthy, active, biodiverse eco-system. They are working to expand existing woodlands, clear streams, create wildlife corridors and improve landscapes.

Coppicing is an ancient tradition with environmental as well as human benefits. In rotation, deciduous trees are cut to a stump, allowing new shoots to grow. This is done on anything from an eight to a 25 year cycle, depending on the predominance of particular tree species. It prolongs the lives of trees, as is demonstrated by a coppiced ash tree at Bradfield Woods which has reached 16 feet in diameter and is believed to be over a thousand years old. A few trees are left standing and seedlings from these are able to become established in the additional light and space between the coppiced trees. Wild flowers and plants are also encouraged by the light and are at their best in the second and third summers after coppicing, after which they decline with the increasing shade. For the endangered dormouse, a hazel, ten to twelve years after coppicing is the ideal habitat. At Bradfield they leave some dead timber for the tree creepers, nuthatch and woodpeckers. Rotational coppicing ensures that different areas of the woods remain at different stages, each of which is ideal for a different range of plants, insects, birds and animals. In Bradfield Woods around 300 species of plants have been identified.

© Anglian Woodland Project

Although Bradfield is unique in the length of time it has been managed the same way and in the protection being a nature reserve affords it, it is a benchmark showing the range of species it is possible to work towards. It is used as a research base by people as diverse as A-level students, post-graduates and the Commonwealth Forestry Association, whose research often has important implications for future woodland management policies.

A major problem for coppiced woodland is the growth in the deer population which browse on new shoots and seedlings. Few people admiring grazing deer or sheep are aware that their growth in numbers is threatening the natural regeneration of the landscape. Pete Fordham and Cathy Harmer, warden and assistant warden at Bradfield Woods, know that they have to control deer, sheep and grey squirrel to maintain population balances. A local deer stalker keeps the deer population down and also has an educative role, encouraging local landowners to support his work, both for the sake of Bradfield and other woodlands, as deer travel over wide areas. Woven fences, made from the unsaleable tops of coppiced wood, protect particularly vulnerable new growth for the first few years after coppicing.

Of particular importance to wildlife is the shorter growth on the rides and ride edges. Where coppicing has been neglected for a long time, other forms of management can be encouraged, such as high oak or ash forest, and if the rides are well managed a diverse range of species will still be encouraged. Maintaining rides demands careful managing of the work of the woodlands. Big machinery may damage them, particularly in wet weather and size of machinery, tyre width and timing of moving heavy loads to coincide with drier periods all have to be considered.

Bob explained that encouraging the management of existing woodland is far more effective than replanting because intensive farming has created far greater ecological damage than has occurred in woodlands suffering from neglect, so the transition to new woodland is a slow process compared to management, natural regeneration and new planting adjacent to existing woods.

Supplying locally grown woodland products also has environmen-tal significance. Bradfields Wood sells firewood, fencing and pea sticks to local people which covers 60% of the costs of managing the woods and reduces transport pollution and the use of imported wood. Although Bradfields Wood can only have a small effect, it would be significant if it was replicated by more woodlands.

The Anglian Woodland Project encouraged the setting up of the British Charcoal Group in 1994, to support and develop the production of British charcoal. Britain currently imports 95% of the 50,000 tons used here annually, most of it on household barbecues. British woodlands could supply a far higher percentage and the Charcoal Group began negotiations with several chain stores to open outlets for their product. These foundered because the big chains wanted central purchasing and distribution which went against the aims of the group. As Bob said, their refusal to accept any terms shook the companies a bit – it was like David setting conditions with Goliath! The big breakthrough came when B&Q, who were already investigating the environmental implications of their products, agreed to a pilot project in which two stores marketed locally produced charcoal. It was a great success and in 1995 the Charcoal Group received a contract to supply 29 stores throughout the country direct from local burners.

As Bob explained, labels on wood products which say they are from sustainably managed sources are often misleading. What they don't say is that the replacement trees planted are often non-native species like pine and that it is not the number of trees that is important but the eco-systems they support. B&Q have recognised this problem and have sent representatives worldwide to investigate the conditions under which wood they purchase has been grown. Their contract with the Charcoal Group will mean that people are able to buy a locally produced product made from raw materials from a local, sustainably managed, broadleaf woodland.

How does it affect the people involved?

 As Bob said, those who are already enlightened like what the project is doing. The challenge is reaching the other owners who are happy with the grain subsidies they are getting and are not concerned about their small patches of woodland. Project workers are talking to land owners directly to dispel the myths and to interest them in managing their own woodland. They find that if they involve and inform owners, talk with them and not at them and 'hold their hand' while they are attempting to establish new practices, most will respond. Bob is aware that mail shots have little effect and that the long, slow process of personal contact is the only way to progress. Although their woodlands will probably not make them money, they can be self supporting and if well managed will increase the capital value of their land.

Management can also improve conditions for sporting use, such as pheasant shooting, which is of interest and financial benefit to many farmers. Bob stressed that although they do not discourage sport because good sporting management is often also good for conservation, the conservation element is their priority. Conservation demands a long term view and as shooting tenancies are often only for three years, they may have different

© Anglian
Woodland
Project

priorities. Bob sees it all as a process of education about the long term interests of the land and the owner.

The Anglian Woodland Project is an example of co-operation and resource sharing among a remarkable range of organisations and individuals, all of whom, according to Bob, are unanimous about what they are trying to achieve. In addition to the core funding group, there is support on the steering group from the National Farmers Union, the Country Landowners Association, the Ministry of Agriculture, English Nature and the British Trust for Conservation Volunteers. The consultation process is even wider, including well attended wood users' meetings, meetings with specialists like the hurdle makers, coppicers and the Charcoal Group, and face to face interviews with a statistical sample of landowners. As Bob says, the Project doesn't presume to know all the answers so they need the opinions of those closer to the action, who recognise local differences. Although farmers don't expect to gain income from their woods, they don't want them to be an expense either. If they manage them individually, it will not be cost effective, but the Project is stressing the benefits of co-operation between landowners in the same area.

There is a great need for more small, commercial businesses in East Anglia. With the emphasis on mechanisation in farming, there has been little recruitment, leading to an ageing, diminishing workforce. Woodland management can create skilled jobs. For example, the gradual drift away from chemically treated softwoods for garden fencing as environmental awareness has grown, has lead to a shortfall of hazel hurdles on the British market, which coppiced woodlands could fill. This in turn would lead to a demand for skilled hurdle makers. Bob believes there could be a wide range of jobs created by woodland management, including linking resources and services, surveying species, cutting, making, marketing and distribution. A by-product of this job creation would be biodiverse and sustainable woodlands.

Bob stresses the chicken-and-egg nature of developing markets, which can only be developed initially through the public sector. He pointed out that if long term production capacity can be forecast, industry can then plan and invest accordingly in sawmills, etc. The markets for wood products are there but are happy to import materials that are not easily available from this country, with the consequent effect on jobs and the environment. Bob believes that only the Forestry Commission is in a position to accurately forecast future timber yields and break the cycle.

As well as creating new jobs, support can be offered to existing businesses. In the entrance to Bradfield Woods is a noticeboard which advertises the services of hurdle makers, greenwood workers who can supply locally made garden furniture, woodland contractors and the local pub, whose trade must be increased by the number of visitors to the woods. Charcoal burners have

© *Anglian Woodland Project*

traditionally worked independently but by creating a central group, they are able to support each other by, for example, organising common insurance policies, sharing legal advice about planning consents and even through developing common bagging methods which will raise the standards of the whole system.

The Woodland Project encouraged the National Rivers Authority to use woven hazel mattresses to strengthen East Anglian river banks against flooding. In 1990, this used 15,000 bundles of coppiced wood, which increased to 30,000 in 1991 and 50,000 in 1992. This year, the NRA put the supply of the faggots out to tender, which the Woodland Project did not win. However, Bob is quite happy about this, feeling that he has created a market for coppiced wood products that didn't previously exist.

Bob sees the whole forestry policy as delivering public benefit. This ranges from jobs to the maintenance of biodiversity and improving public recreational access. He is a strong believer in co-operation and open discussion at the earliest stages, feeling that if people are involved from the beginning, their interest is caught and they become a partner and go on to educate others.

Cathy stressed the personal pleasure people gain from having access to diverse woodlands. People say that Bradford Woods is like a green oasis in the middle of a desert of cornfields. They currently have a dozen regular volunteers, some of them retired, supplemented by more occasional helpers, who love being able to spend time in the woods. They enjoy the opportunity to be actively, physically involved in doing something positive for the environment as well as being part of the group. When Pete first started working there, they had problems with local teenagers riding motor bikes through the woods. It hasn't happened for years now and there is no vandalism. Pete questions whether this is due to raised awareness or because of having more people around. Many local landowners are doubtful about encouraging greater public access to their woods, but this seems to demonstrate that larger numbers of visitors can have a beneficial effect on the way people behave.

As part of their educational remit, they encourage opportunities for people to make things on their visits, using materials from the woods. School children make small hurdles that they can take away, sometimes covering them with mud and straw to explore how wattle and daub houses are made. Makers of greenwood furniture have hired a space in the woods to run workshops. These have been very popular, with people wanting to make a piece of furniture for their garden as well as those who are keen to develop a skill. Visitors enjoy watching people using hand tools to make something usable from materials grown on site.

Has participation raised involvement with broader issues?

 Bob believes it has. He gave the example of the Norfolk Forestry Club which began as liaison between farmers and local people who wanted the woodlands preserved from being cut down or damaged by vandals. Gradually they began to realise the potential of improved management and as community spirit and co-operation developed, so did a more active and informed interest in conservation. He sees the Woodland Project as running in parallel to Agenda 21, sharing the same goals of environmental improvement, partnership and jobs.

He returned to the example of B&Q who have changed their internal marketing system to accommodate the Charcoal Group's demands for local sourcing, and suggested that this could influence their approach to supplying other commodities. A problem at the beginning had been an expectation that British charcoal must be priced competitively although it costs more to produce than imported charcoal. This meant a very small profit for the retailer which itself would be unsustainable. Finally they added an arbitrary 50p per bag which, to their surprise, did not affect sales. This demonstrated that not all sales are price-lead. In this case, customers not only found that it was a better product (it reaches higher temperatures more rapidly) but they were also influenced by a desire to do something to support their local environment and local employment. The Charcoal Group's packaging also went against accepted marketing wisdom. A shelf of plain brown paper bags stood out from the competing bright colours around it and customers liked the environmental message given by the lack of bleaching and added pigment, and the use of a biodegradable, renewable material.

The workers at Bradfield Woods are frequently asked about sources for local charcoal by people who have read articles in the national press about the work of the Charcoal Group. Bob, Cathy and Pete all stressed the enthusiasm people have for supporting their local woodland once they are aware of ways in which they can do so. Because there is a regular local wood supply, some residents in the vicinity of Bradfield Woods have made a choice to install woodburning stoves. Cathy believes there is a lack of connectedness about where things come from – that in most people's minds, furniture comes from a factory not a woodland. She believes that by seeing a working woodland people's awareness of process is raised. They become aware that they can buy locally produced things and can also themselves make things from local materials. She believes this can increase people's self reliance. People also see habitat management processes that they may be able to replicate in a small way in their own gardens.

Bob is keen that this awareness of connections and processes should be taken even further. He talked of books on school grounds development which suggest starting with an old railway sleeper instead of saying, 'Go to your local woodland and choose a piece of sweet chestnut'. Most schools plan for grounds developments a year ahead and with forward planning, could feed through such future needs to woodland managers. This would encourage a real understanding of the processes of sustainable development, rather than the traditional preservationist approach of 'We mustn't cut down trees' which is often prevalent in environmental education.

And the downside?

Bob is adamant that development of woodland management must remain in the public sector for at least ten more years, until the private sector infrastructure has built up, but this is threatened due to tightening public purse strings. Countryside Commission funding is currently under question due to Government cuts. The

Local Authorities involved are fully committed to the principles of the project but have to balance this against their statutory obligations towards such things as policing, education and social services. Woodland management schemes in other parts of the country which originally had similar aims have been forced into immediate income generation. This has meant that they have moved away from their original targets and are now concentrating on bigger woodlands which are easier and more rapidly economic to manage. Bob emphasised the fact that the Anglian Woodland Project does not need large inputs of cash to be effective, but it does need trained people with time to set the systems in place and to train others before it can become self supporting.

Bob, Pete and Cathy all stressed the long time scale of their work and the complications of matching demand to supply. They said publicity was easy; many people feel a natural affinity to woodlands and are very enthusiastic about anything which they feel they can do to support their wellbeing. The danger is awakening a demand for local charcoal or wood products which the mechanisms are not yet in place to supply. On the other hand, landowners will not begin to manage their woodlands unless they feel there will be a market for their products and there aren't yet enough contractors with the necessary skills to complete the circle.

With the markets currently being supplied from abroad, Bob argues that appreciation for the need for woodland management must come first from a recognition of the value of the woodlands to society as a whole, which will not be supplied purely by reliance on market forces. The economy of the area the Project covers is driven disproportionately by the Common Agricultural Policy which has a huge budget to support grain production, against which forestry cannot compete in terms of financial incentives. Woodland management demands a more holistic approach to farming, for example recognising the possibilities of sourcing the materials used on the farm from the farm woodland. Bob has no doubt that a reduction in grain subsidies from the CAP would encourage diversification which would be good for woodlands.

Bob feels that users of wood products can influence the market. Retailers will continue to import as long as it makes them profits, unless the customer asks questions about sustainability as well as commercial improvements. Free competition with the cheap labour becoming increasingly available from eastern Europe will mean that retailers will import materials unless the broader picture sustainability demands is recognised. As Cathy said, woodlands demand long-term thinking, which doesn't make a quick buck but develops a sustainable, ongoing resource.

Through Local Agenda 21, Local Authorities could encourage architects, designers and engineers to specify the use of local materials where appropriate. For example, signposts showing public rights of way could be sourced from local woodlands. Bob believes there is a tendency for people to continue unquestioningly with established practices and feels the onus should be on the specifiers to justify current practice. Imported softwoods are often treated with copper, chrome and arsenic, all of them potential pollutants, which would not be needed if British hardwoods were used. Bob believes many materials are overspecified. For example, river defences only need to last about ten years while the banks stabilise as vegetation takes over. Yet often tropical greenheart is used, which lasts for ever. Knot-free wood is unnecessary unless the wood is to be load bearing, but 'psychological marketing' has lead the consumer to demand it. Awareness needs to be raised of sustainability issues throughout the industry.

Public enthusiasm for the woodlands can be a double edged sword, with many people interpreting conservation as not touching anything. As Bob explained, if biodiversity is to be maintained, non-intervention is not an option – the result would be an ageing, non-regenerating woodland, gradually taken over by invasive species. The idea of culling deer is also anathema to many people with a love of nature and it will be a major education process to convince people that the natural balance has been irrevocably changed, and that deer thrive at the expense of young trees and of other less prolific species. Some supporters of Bradfield Woods have an instinctive reaction against the removal of any trees, even when it will enhance natural regeneration.

Some people also dislike the idea of more visitors coming to the woods. Bob considers improved access to woods is vital, benefiting the community and increasing awareness. However, the workers at Bradfield Woods, while supporting this viewpoint, are very aware that with increasing publicity, the pressure of numbers could be too great and research is being carried out about the number of visitors the woodland can carry without severe damage to the ecosystem. Pete is asking questions about whether they should increase the car parking spaces (currently the only way people living too far away to walk or cycle can visit is by car, polluting the countryside en route) or whether it would be viable to negotiate with the local bus company for more frequent services. The popularity of Bradfields shows the need for more local woodlands to be opened to the public to take pressure off a few well-publicised sites.

Cathy sounded a final word of caution. Although awareness of the value of woodlands is increasing, and after fifty years of decline there has been a net increase in woodlands since the late 1980s, many of them are planted with little awareness of the ecosystems they support. The ancient woodlands and hedgerows with their enormous biodiversity are irreplaceable in the same way as the rainforests are, and they are still being lost due to new roads and farming practices.

City Lands Redevelopment

City Lands is a redevelopment that is attempting to tackle "the deep seated problems of physical, economic and social decline in Central Birkenhead and the area around the docks". (*City Lands Annual Report*, 1992–93). It covers an area of four or five square miles, including 28,000 people.

It is a City Challenge project, with a remit to improve the city centre and tempt in businesses. However, this particular scheme places novel emphasis on developing approaches that will "give residents a sense of hope, belonging and safety in their own environment through special initiatives to reduce the fear of crime, improve health and strengthen community spirit".

Because this is a complex, many-faceted project, this case study is divided into two sections. The first gives an overview of the project. The second is a more detailed account of the neighbourhood colleges, an important and particularly successful aspect of the redevelopment.

AN OVERVIEW

How did it happen?

? The Metropolitan Borough of Wirral won a competition to become a City Challenge area. This brought in Government funding for a period of five years, designed to lever in additional private and public sector investment.

The aims for the project include:

- making City Lands a better place for everyone who lives in and visits the area

- ensuring a cleaner and healthier environment for all
- developing the existing communities by helping them to work together within the Community Action Network
- developing training opportunities so that City Lands residents can be better trained to take advantage of the opportunities achieved through the Wirral Investment Network
- providing a safer environment for the vulnerable members of the community.

The task has been to fulfil this imaginative vision of improving quality of life for all residents, within the constraints imposed by a Government quango, including the time scale of five years. Its success was likely to depend on the amount of real public consultation and involvement it achieved.

A Community Action Network (CAN) was set up, with a wide membership of affiliated local groups. Elected representatives from each neighbourhood are responsible for allocating the community projects budget to ensure that the priorities of each neighbourhood are met, and CAN also has representation on the main funding committee.

Maureen Corish, one of the community representatives, began her community involvement in 1987, as a street representative on a tenants' association, negotiating with the Council and contractors over improvement schemes in her street. People were relocated temporarily during the work and it was during this process that Maureen became aware of the depths of hidden poverty in the area, and began helping people to access the support to which they were entitled. She talked of early mistakes and the steep learning curve she went through which lead to her being 'headhunted' for CAN.

CAN's first action was to commission a survey which went to all households in the City Lands area, to find out the views of residents towards issues that could be influenced by the initiative. This had the double function of a marketing exercise and information gathering. Over 2,000 surveys were returned; an 18% response rate which, according to Val Machin, Project Manager for City Lands, makes them 'brand leaders' being far higher than the 2% return they had been told to expect. This was supplemented by more specific surveys providing detailed information about employment, shopping facilities and schools. The survey showed that the worst features in the area were perceived to be employment and training opportunities, leisure facilities, community centres, childcare provision and the physical environment. It also found that needs and priorities varied across the area.

Maureen says, "Selling City Lands was selling a promise and you've got to remember that people have been made lots of promises by lots of governments before and seen nothing for it." So CAN decided to make a few noticeable changes, such as improving play facilities in local parks and doing up shopfronts in core areas. They then talked to people using the facilities, asking if they knew that the improvements were funded by City Lands money and what else they would like to see changed. That is when people started coming to them.

Maureen believes community participation happens through providing facilities that people want. She says no-one turns up to meetings, but pensioners' bingo nights provide an opportunity to talk about people's real problems and needs. She is a trustee of Wallasey Neighbourhood Resource Centre (see Neighbourhood Colleges, below) which runs a savings club to fund trips to Blackpool and York at affordable prices for people on income support. Once they have come on a trip, people find out about other things that are going on.

There are legal problems with using City Lands money to create jobs for local people. The Council are prohibited by the 1989 Local Government Act from specifying that companies they contract should employ local people. The Treaty of Rome gives all European citizens the right to work anywhere, so City Lands building projects draw workers from far afield. However, a commitment has been negotiated with local businesses that they will advertise in the neighbourhood colleges and community centres a week before advertising more widely and that appropriate people with City Lands addresses will be guaranteed interviews. City Lands will also give employers a contribution to the salary of a local person for the first year, on condition that it is a permanent post. If local applicants don't have the appropriate skills, information is fed back to the colleges so that they can set up courses in relevant skills. With the building of a new swimming pool, courses have been set up in lifeguard and first aid training, so that local people will stand a chance of getting one of the new jobs.

Maureen talked of the problem of loan sharks charging high interest rates in poor areas where people have no other access to credit. Credit unions had been set up in a small way by local churches, but City Lands money has paid for them to take on shopfront premises, which make it easier for them to promote their services. The credit unions are non-profit making and only charge 2% interest on loans, which they hope will pay a member of staff to support volunteers and enable them to continue after the end of City Lands. Maureen explained that they help people to manage their money, giving bigger loans to people who have saved regularly for some months. People take out loans for Christmas or to pay for funerals. The credit unions have been so successful that Maureen's network of contacts tell her there are no longer loan sharks operating on the estates involved.

To satisfy the need for affordable childcare, as well as providing crèches in the neighbourhood colleges, an important initiative has been the appointment of a Childminder Development Worker within City Lands. Her job is to help prospective childminders through the maze of red-tape that they have to circumvent before being able to offer a much needed service that is in short supply in the area.

Alcohol abuse among the young concerns many people. The Wallasey Centre is installing a non-alcoholic bar with computer and arcade games. Maureen believes this provision will remove the need to steal money to play the arcades as well as providing places other than pubs for young people to meet.

A new Well Woman Clinic and Brook Advisory Centre are attempting to tackle the ill-health and teenage pregnancies which are far higher in City Lands than in the rest of Wirral, supplemented by the Leaders in Fitness and Exercise Project (LIFE) which is encouraging the adoption of a healthier lifestyle through mobile fitness testing, the provision of new sports facilities and community health courses such as an activity club for the over 50s, with free mini-bus transport provision for all City Lands residents. LIFE has also trained and employed local people as fitness instructors and health advice workers. A collaboration between Leisure and Health Services recompenses doctors who, in appropriate cases, dispense free passes for the swimming pool instead of prescriptions. Leisure Services have made a commitment to continue the scheme beyond the life of City Lands.

How does it help the environment?

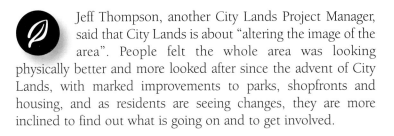

Jeff Thompson, another City Lands Project Manager, said that City Lands is about "altering the image of the area". People felt the whole area was looking physically better and more looked after since the advent of City Lands, with marked improvements to parks, shopfronts and housing, and as residents are seeing changes, they are more inclined to find out what is going on and to get involved.

CAN funds small scale projects that reflect residents' priorities, which have included traffic calming in residential streets and tidying up derelict areas. It has funded changes on housing estates: for example, one estate which was suffering badly from burglaries has had alleyways blocked off, leaving only one entrance, making strangers more noticeable.

Although visual improvements are easier to achieve, some attempt has been made to limit environmental damage as well. Pressure through CAN has managed to prevent businesses that would cause pollution from moving into the area. An incinerator was planned which it was said would spread carcinogenic toxins over a wide area. Regardless of the jobs it would have provided, people from the area got together and stopped it happening. As Maureen said, "Jobs are important but not at the expense of risks to the local community."

There have also been improvements to transport including the provision of a new railway station and tramway and a network of footpaths and cycle routes, though some people suggested these are all clustered at one end of the area, around the town centre redevelopment, and have little impact on most residents although they may improve the prospects of local businesses.

How has it affected the people involved?

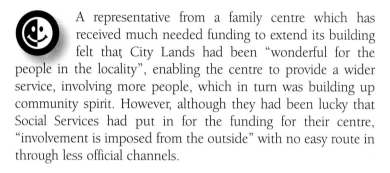 A representative from a family centre which has received much needed funding to extend its building felt that City Lands had been "wonderful for the people in the locality", enabling the centre to provide a wider service, involving more people, which in turn was building up community spirit. However, although they had been lucky that Social Services had put in for the funding for their centre, "involvement is imposed from the outside" with no easy route in through less official channels.

Maureen is quite clear that City Lands money has given the area a way to tackle problems they'd have only been able to nibble at otherwise, providing resources and bringing people together to talk about solutions. She stressed the importance of CAN in the process of getting value for money in the community projects. As she says, "No-one can con the community if it's the community that are actually doing it. Anyone coming into a community with a lot of money to help an area goes back at the end of the day to where they live. We don't go away. We love the area we work in. There's got to be real community involvement – the community have to be seen to be doing it."

Val believes City Lands has made a great difference to people directly benefiting from innovations such as improved street lighting, and free personal alarm systems for those who feel vulnerable and can't afford the Council scheme. She acknowledged that, "If you went into the street and stopped the first ten people you met, you probably wouldn't get one who knew anything about City Lands, but most people couldn't name their ward councillor either." This was borne out by a taxi driver who said, "All these signposts appeared saying City Lands and nobody knows what it is!" However, he did admit to having noticed a definite improvement in the state of the local shops. Val believes that there will be a knock on effect through the people who have become involved, who will be able to spearhead future developments. In the long term, she hopes that "We'll have started a process" which could lead to a more active, better informed and educated population who are beginning to believe that they can have an effect.

Has participation raised involvement with broader issues?

 The CAN committee is setting up a Wirral-wide federation of tenants associations to discuss solutions to common problems. Maureen's experiences have led her to go to Housing Associations and insist that they provide accommodation for elderly people within new residencies, rather than in separate developments. Members of the committee are advising other areas who are applying for City Challenge money about ways of building up community representation.

Wirral is about to receive money from Objective 1, a European fund, which has been obtained because City Lands money was accepted as matching funding. With City Lands, because of the timescale, the draft action plan was prepared before the community were involved, which caused some resentment and suspicion of motives. A condition of Objective 1 funding is that it must be community lead and people from the community have been involved since the inception. City Lands has begun community participation and made it easier to develop the process with Objective 1. A CAN worker is now based at Central Birkenhead Neighbourhood College, funded by City Lands to ensure that every group in the community has a say in how Objective 1 funding is spent.

Interestingly, Local Agenda 21 has had little impact on City Lands. City Lands is independent from the Council and covers only one part of Wirral, whereas Agenda 21 is an authority-wide issue. However, project workers are doubtful as to whether Local Agenda 21 can achieve much without additional funding in an authority which is having difficulty in financing its statutory obligations. They thought that the Council saw Groundwork (another Government quango) as a route to participation and also placed faith in existing, articulate local conservation groups.

And the downside?

Although there are obvious success stories, particularly with regard to the physical regeneration of the area, almost everyone I spoke to had some reservations about the City Lands process. Ward councillors have not been included in decision making at board or local level, which project managers feel has made it harder for them to do their jobs effectively, increasing resentment of what is perceived to be an unelected, unaccountable quango. No-one was prepared to commit themselves as to why this had happened, but the suggestion was made that it was on civil service advice. Maureen says that anyone getting involved in such a scheme must be aware of the dangers of Government departments intimidating the community. "If the community say no to something and give valid reasons for saying no, it shouldn't happen. The only way to regenerate an area is on a local level." Certainly, if local people do not feel that their needs have been responded to, improvements will be short lived.

Further grounds for cynicism was the belief that businesses will move from one area to another to follow the grants, so that no new jobs are created, just relocation of the old ones. This can also apply to shops which may move to be within the area eligible for facelifts, increasing dereliction in other areas. City Challenge funding is not new money. It is all taken from existing budgets and the element of competition means that there are loosers as well as winners. City Challenge boundaries come from a planners map and therefore exclude people in need who happen to live on the wrong side of the road.

Long term change may be difficult to bring about in the time scale of only five years to complete projects before funding ceases and the project team moves on. Physical improvements requiring one-off capital grants are easier to achieve. Projects that are up and running in the first year can be given tapering revenue funding, which may give them time to develop long term maintenance strategies; but as time progresses, anything funded has to be rapidly self supporting. The family centre which had its building extended has no money for additional staffing and relies on volunteers to maximise use of the space.

Access to information has been made harder by the fact that community groups have found themselves working with six or seven different Council departments in order to develop one project. Local Government officers may not be experienced in working with community participation and project workers felt that they need to be offered training

City Challenge funding, unlike European Objective 1 funding, does not require that projects should be community lead. It is credit to some committed workers and volunteers in City Lands that there has been participation, but it has been patchy. Uptake of services has been much better around existing community centres, where paid workers were available to inform people about the possibilities, but very limited in areas with no history of participation. Val suggested that those benefiting most were people in "the next layer up from the most disadvantaged" because when suffering extreme levels of stress, people are less able to access opportunities. She said that opportunities have to be provided for participation at a comfortable level for each individual and that too much responsibility too early can be as disempowering as too little.

For real participation to take place, it was suggested that a two year lead-in is needed before money begins to be spent on projects – as against the six month consultation period required by Objective 1. However much work is put into marketing, it seems that the only really effective means of spreading involvement is by word of mouth. For City Lands, consultants were employed to run community meetings. This failed, as any of the local people involved could have told them it would. As the worker of the family centre which has over 1,000 users said, "External meetings don't work, people are too afraid to attend. They should have come here to say to our users what do *you* want and why?"

The CAN committee worked valiantly on behalf of their communities, but a small number of overworked volunteers, usually heavily involved in running their own projects, were inevitably unable to keep local people sufficiently informed. It was suggested that a priority should have been the appointment of local community development workers who would be out in pubs and play groups making sure that everyone had the opportunity to be heard. This may not sit easily within regeneration budgets which are expected to deliver tangible outcomes, but as Val said, £1 million pounds spent on a team of development workers over five years would not make a large hole in a total investment of £212 million.

Despite these limitations, three years on, City Lands has definitely begun the long, slow process of empowerment for a significant number of people who may be catalysts for future community action. There is much to learn from this project and, if listened to, the experience of people here could lead to more effective approaches by future funding initiatives. Hopefully the people of City Lands may themselves reap the rewards of their growing experience through the second chance they are being given with Objective 1 funding, to work towards lasting change in Wirral.

THE NEIGHBOURHOOD COLLEGES

How did it happen?

The four new Neighbourhood Colleges are unique to City Lands. Wirral Metropolitan College provides further and higher education for 30,000 students from all over the country, but for people who failed at school a large institution some distance away may be an insurmountable barrier. The College had the innovative idea of applying for City Lands money to ensure that everyone has a centre within a mile of home.

Central Birkenhead Neighbourhood College is in a shopfront near the post office, the chemist, the chip shop and the launderette. As well as encouraging casual callers, the workers go out during the summer break and leaflet the 4,500 households within their zone. Although the leaflets themselves have limited effect, being

on the street delivering them provides the workers with opportunities to talk directly to people about what they have to offer. Claire Vickers, the Manager, says "We are taking education to the people rather than expecting them to come to us and I think that has been one of the major successes – we're accessible, we're on people's doorsteps."

Paul McGovern, the Neighbourhood Worker, sees an important element of their success as being that the workers are from the community. He and Claire are both 'second chancers' who failed at school themselves. Paul came straight to the job from a production line and is now half way through a B. Tech. He believes he can achieve things in the area that a trained manager or lecturer couldn't do. "You end up being a kind of role model for people because you come from the same environment and background as them. You're not seen as someone with an academic background, coming from outside the area and telling them what to do."

Claire stressed the holistic approach of the neighbourhood colleges. Careers advice, a crèche, a health worker and a CAN worker are based there so that students don't have to make appointments to see different people in different buildings. Because they're small organisations, they can offer a personal service. They have far lower drop out rates than the main sites, as well as high recruitment. Claire says that there's a real sense of ownership among the students in the neighbourhood colleges that isn't there on the main sites. Students call back regularly after they have finished their courses to use the equipment and facilities or to ask advice. Community meetings are held there and a noticeboard advertises local events and services.

The way the neighbourhood colleges approach their role puts the participants in control. Claire says they can't promise people qualifications which will lead to jobs, because the jobs may not be there. The emphasis is on personal development. The workers try to provide courses that will mean something to the local community – like welfare rights and politics – that could lead to GCSE sociology, government or politics, but will be useful in their everyday lives if they choose not to progress to academic qualifications. They have recently carried out a questionnaire so that they can provide evidence that the kinds of courses they are offering are demand lead.

Claire believes Wirral Metropolitan College has been very courageous to try the neighbourhood approach when other colleges are centralising for financial reasons. "We're doing the opposite and we've had fantastic results." City Lands enabled them to take the risk, funding building conversions and salaries for a limited time, so that the College could measure the success of the idea before taking on permanent funding themselves.

The Wallasey Neighbourhood Resource Centre hires out rooms to other organisations and hopes that by the end of City Lands, they will be self financing. Business managers have helped them to draw up a business plan. Maureen stressed the importance of such partnership approaches. She says it is on the community that the future of the project will depend, but it is also important to involve representatives from local businesses in joint management to share their experience of efficient ways of working.

How does it help the environment?

Paul believes that the high quality of work that went into redeveloping the Community College buildings both upgrades the area and emphasises the worth of the students. The number of people using the colleges brings more life to the areas in which they are situated. Because of the sense of local ownership the neighbourhood colleges encourage, they have had no vandalism, although it is a major problem at the main site colleges. People have been reluctant to invest in the area, but Claire believes that City Lands funding has proved that money spent well, responding to the real needs of the community, will be respected.

How has it affected the people involved?

Paul believes that whatever you do to the buildings and the traffic schemes, what really improves the quality of life for people living in an area is making them feel good about themselves and giving them more self esteem. Many people in Wirral left school with very low expectations but the neighbourhood colleges are changing that, giving people the belief that they can succeed. Seven people in the GCSE Sociology group achieved the highest grades in the whole of Wirral College and three of these are now on Access to Higher Education courses with an option to go on to University. Claire sees the improvements in self esteem as being as important as improvements in basic skills when it comes to success in the job market. She suggested that if parents take control of their own learning, it will also affect their children's expectations and motivation.

Maureen also feels that the self confidence of people taking courses at the colleges is greatly increasing. She is delighted to have proved wrong those who said that people in her area wouldn't be interested in being educated. There are now waiting lists for most of the courses, including GNVQs in maths, English, French, computing and desk-top publishing. Over 1,000 people a week use the Wallasey Centre. She says it wasn't education people were against, but having to spend time and money on travelling when they are on low incomes. She talks of the pride people who failed at school feel about getting qualifications.

Paid work is the one factor that would make most difference to many people in the City Lands area. Neighbourhood College workers are hopeful that training plus environmental improvements may lever in businesses as the third part of the jigsaw. They said that people's postal address could be a stigma which automatically excluded them from many jobs, but that proof of good quality training in the area may help to overcome this.

Has participation raised involvement with broader issues?

 Claire said that the added confidence and communication skills people develop through attending the College enables them to participate in all sorts of things they wouldn't previously have felt were for them. People leave college feeling empowered to ask questions and to make their opinion heard, and she gave several examples of students getting involved with broader issues. The writing course included writing to an MP about an issue of local concern. Some students sent their letters, and a reply on House of Commons notepaper made them feel their views had been taken notice of. Another practical exercise had lead to students writing to the local paper about the proposed imposition of VAT on books, asking people to consider the effect this would have on them and their children.

Central Birkenhead Neighbourhood College runs a specific course on communication skills, which includes speaking effectively at meetings. This was used to great effect against a non-smoking policy which was going to be imposed by the main College. Neighbourhood College students secured a meeting with the deputy principal and through rational and structured arguments, won concessions. The ban will now be postponed for a year, during which time courses on stopping smoking and relaxation techniques will be offered to those who want them. The students union has a representative on the Wirral College committee which gives the students some say in how money is allocated. A student union representative also attends City Lands meetings.

And the downside?

Much of the success of the neighbourhood colleges has been due to the participatory approach of the workers. People coming into the centre often have a history of unemployment stretching over ten to fifteen years and, as Paul says, "It's not enough to enrol them, fill in the form and think you've finished. It takes a person-centred approach to help people who've had so much taken away from them – to put anything back is a long process." However, Government funding is for skills training and this is the angle the Colleges focus on in their reports. Their more holistic approach is something they maintain despite, rather than because of, funding criteria. Claire talked of the "increasingly hard task of balancing funding and empowerment, product and process…" but said philosophically, "We're working to different agendas, but maybe as local people we can fulfil the funders' aims and our own".

There seems to be a question about whether women find it easier to benefit from these kind of community developments than men do. A low proportion of people taking up neighbourhood college courses are men. Paul saw this as having something to do with the self perceptions of men in the area. He suggested they feel they should be the family breadwinners. The older men are highly skilled and qualified to work in the now defunct shipyards and don't want to go back to learning new skills from scratch. The younger men, often second or third generation unemployed, can't see the point in education unless there's a job at the end. Women, on the other hand, see the free crèche places as time off from the kids, enjoy the contact and improved self esteem and once there, often move on.

Synopses of the case studies

Segal Self Build

Walter Segal was an architect who pioneered a system of timber frame building which was simple enough to be built by people with no previous building skills. A trust has been set up in his name to support people, especially those on low incomes and in housing need, to build decent homes for themselves. New developments are usually financed through Housing Associations and are often built by people from Council waiting lists. They are low cost, covering only the cost of land and materials, the labour being provided by those who will live in the houses.

The houses are built above the ground on 'pad' foundations, meaning that they can be built on sloping sites, among mature trees, causing minimal disturbance to the environment. Some of the developments have turf roofs. The frames are made from soft-wood from sustainable sources, and stains and emulsions are organic and non-toxic. The design of the houses makes the most of passive solar heating and they are well insulated, with very low energy requirements.

The process of self build creates co-operative, stable communities which have taken responsibility for their own environment. Participants experience a sense of achievement and an increase in confidence at the same time as developing building and negotiating skills. At the end, they have high quality housing at a low rent, making it easier for them to support themselves without state assistance.

A possible threat to self build is the reduction of public money available to Housing Associations and the reluctance of private sources to fund anything out-of-the-ordinary. Participants have also experienced a reluctance on the part of architects, site managers and Housing Associations to give control to the builders, without which there is little incentive for them to give such a large part of their lives to the building process.

Local Exchange Trading Systems (LETS)

The LETS system is a form of barter credit club. It is a community based initiative to tackle poverty and improve quality of life. Members use a local directory to advertise their own skills and to locate people with skills they need. Work is paid for through a cheque book based on a local currency. Personal accounts are debited and can be balanced later by providing goods or services for someone else.

The advantages of LETS currency over normal money is that it gives instant access to interest free credit and can thus help to keep people out of debt and allow needs to be met as they arise, before they reach crisis proportions. It stays local, unlike 'real' money which tends to bleed from poor areas to rich ones. It has environmental benefits, using fewer non-human resources. Labour is cheaper than materials, therefore goods are repaired, exchanged and loaned. The local provision of goods and services reduces transportation needs.

The system also has the advantage of helping to build a sense of community. It often provides higher quality goods and services as people are working for their neighbours and goods are hand made or locally grown. It has helped people with mental health problems, providing for immediate needs without money worries, cutting through social isolation and increasing feelings of self worth.

Members have access to goods such as freezer meals, grown and prepared on a local smallholding; services such as decorating, baby sitting and gardening; and training in anything from computer skills to cheese making. One person built a house using LETS labour, and paid off his debt within six months instead of 30 years of mortgage repayments. There are now over 200 local LETS in Britain.

The only threat to the system is the possibility that the success of LETS schemes in reducing dependency on high-interest loans, in an economy which makes big profits from such practices, may lead to legislation which makes their continuation difficult. Already, some unemployed people are afraid that involvement in the scheme might lead to premature cuts in benefits.

Larchfield Community

This is a community inspired by the ideas of Rudolf Steiner, in which about 40 people, many with learning difficulties, live and work. Training and employment are also provided for non-residents in a bakery, woodwork and weaving workshops, a market garden, a cafe and the farm. Farming methods are organic and all sewage is treated biologically through a series of ponds and reed beds which create a rich wetland habitat. Larchfield is financed through sales of farm produce and craft work, training fees and the social security payments received by the special needs residents.

The community is run by a series of committees which reach decisions by debating until consensus is reached. Great importance is placed on the recognition of every individual's needs and abilities, stressing self reliance and interdependence, rather than self sufficiency. No-one receives wages but everyone has food and shelter and can draw on a communal fund for personal needs such as clothing and holidays. Day workers are paid according to their own assessment of their needs. The community exists on a basis of trust but everyone can see the results of their actions and the importance of their contribution.

Larchfield are aware of the danger of having to shape their training work to fit the requirements of the funders, which are often affected by changing Government priorities. There is an increasing pressure for rapid 'throughput' of trainees, which goes against the Larchfield belief that training must continue until the recipient feels confident to do the job. The benefits system prevents unemployed volunteers from working more than a limited number of hours without losing benefits. Larchfield tends to have different values to the world outside, which may make it hard for residents, particularly children, to cope with life outside the community.

Biological water treatment systems are unlikely to come into common use in this country without a change in legislation. Only statutory water companies have access to grants to set up sewage treatment systems and developers would have to pay to install such systems, whereas connection to the mains costs them nothing.

The Anglian Woodland Project

This project is based on the premise that the decline of British broadleaved woodlands will only be halted when the ideal of preserving and improving existing woodlands for their wildlife and conservation value is combined with rural job creation and the provision of an economic incentive for good management. Demand for British broadleaved timber is currently considerably less than potential supply.

The Forestry Commission has joined with the Countryside Commission and four County Councils to raise awareness of the desirability of bringing the 78% of small woodlands which are unmanaged back into management and to provide incentives and development programmes to help it to happen. Landowners are given advice and helped to find markets for their wood. The project believes that management can create a wide range of jobs in linking resources and services, surveying species, cutting, making, marketing and distribution.

The traditional technique of coppicing is being revived, with trees being cut on an eight to a 25 year cycle. Coppicing prolongs the lives of trees, creates a diverse habitat and generates marketable wood every year. The project is working with charcoal burners to develop the local charcoal industry. Currently 95% of charcoal burned in this country is imported. As part of this process, they have persuaded B&Q to stock British charcoal in 29 of their stores, supplied direct by local burners.

The project aims to hand over work created to the private sector, but believes that only the public sector is able to raise awareness, set standards and put systems into place. The ten years it believes this process will take is threatened by tightening public purse strings. The Common Agricultural Policy has a huge budget to support grain production against which forestry cannot compete in financial terms. Workers are acutely aware of the complications of matching demand to supply. Publicity may encourage markets to move from imported to British goods, but there may not yet be enough contractors with the necessary skills to supply them. On the other hand, contractors will not set up until they know there is a market. Conservation movements sometimes undermine woodland regeneration, discouraging any cutting of trees and working against anyone who recommends culling the deer which are currently destroying all new growth.

City Lands, Wirral

City Lands is a redevelopment project that is attempting to tackle "the deep seated problems of physical, economic and social decline in Central Birkenhead and the area around the docks" (*City Lands Annual Report*, 1992–93). As well as building new shops and offices, City Lands is providing a mixture of low cost housing and improving transport by the provision of a new railway station and tramway, a network of footpaths and cycle routes and a 'shopmobility' scheme with motorised wheelchairs and scooters for people with disabilities. The development of low-interest credit unions has wiped loan sharks from nearby estates.

Emphasis is placed on developing approaches that will "give residents a sense of hope, belonging and safety in their own environment through special initiatives to reduce the fear of crime, improve health and strengthen community spirit". The consultation process has involved questionnaires to all local households and shopkeepers, and the formation of a Community Action Network (CAN) through which local representatives oversee the development process, ensuring that the priorities of their neighbourhood are included.

An innovative approach to training has been developed by Wirral Metropolitan College which has set up four neighbourhood colleges so that all City Lands residents have a centre within a mile of home. Central Birkenhead Neighbourhood College is in a shopfront and as well as encouraging casual callers, local people are employed as neighbourhood workers to encourage people to use the facilities. A crèche, careers advice, a health worker and a CAN worker are all based there. The personal approach and sense of ownership experienced by students has encouraged high recruitment and low drop-out rates.

City Challenge funding is not new money but is taken from other budgets, so there are losers as well as winners. There is a possibility that shops and businesses will move from one area to another to follow the grants, creating greater dereliction elsewhere. Funding is only for five years, meaning that it is easier to fund capital expenditure than running costs and new projects must become rapidly self supporting. The reliance on overstretched volunteers means that consultation has been patchy. Uptake of services and resources has been best around existing community centres but limited in areas with no history of participation. Government funding to colleges is for skills training. The Community Colleges feel that they maintain their more holistic approach, with its emphasis on process as well as product, despite rather than because of funding criteria.

PART 3

Follow up

Key questions about the transition to sustainability

As I researched the case studies certain issues seemed to recur, raising a number of questions about the transition to sustainability. For me, these were:

- Can only small scale, grass roots projects be fully sustainable?

- What is the role of small, grass roots projects:
  – Are they only of value to the people involved or do they have an wider educational value?
  – How can their ideas and experiences be disseminated?
  – Are they sustainable in the long term if they are not supported by a broader movement?
  – Can they help us to achieve sustainability on a global scale?

- What should the relationship be between grass roots initiatives, Government policy and financial institutions, for sustainability to be realised?

- How can projects be sustained over the long time scales necessary to develop real participation within a system where funders and politicians require a short term pay-back ?

● What processes will men and women have to go through to contribute equally to and benefit equally from sustainable development?

● How can development happen at a speed that individuals and communities can maintain control over?

● How can the cycle of increasing working hours for those in employment be broken and fear of reduction in benefits for the unemployed be removed, in order for people to

More thoughts on sustainability

"I can imagine a biocommunity thriving well without any human members but I cannot imagine human society thriving without a well functioning biocommunity. Similarly, I can imagine human society function-ing well without a given individual but I cannot imagine an individual thriving without a well-functioning human community. Therefore, indi-viduals requiring quality of life must give top priority to protection and preservation of their biocommunity (their ecosystem). Second priority must go to preservation and protec-tion of the good functioning of their social community. Only when people are careful to protect the viability of their two communities is it acceptable for individuals to pursue quality of life according to their own personal desires."

(Lester W Milbrath, *Envisioning a Sustainable Society*, 1989)

"The well-being of a community of people working together becomes greater the less each individual demands for himself the products of his own achievements; that is, the more of those products he passes on to his fellow workers and the more his own needs are satisfied not out of his own achievements but out of the achievements of others."

(The Fundamental Social Law of Rudolph Steiner, 1919. From a lecture series 'The Social Question')

"You have to look at each individual situation for the most appropriate solution. The idea that one construction form is right or wrong is just plain stupid. You have to weigh the alternatives."

(Chris Hudson, Iris Water, in conversation, 1995)

participate fully in efforts to improve quality of life in their families and neighbourhoods?

- What is the relationship between social well-being and sustainable resource use? Although improved street lighting may help perceptions of safety and environmental quality it will contribute to environmental pollution.
  – How can people's immediate needs be reconciled with the long-term needs of the planet?
  – Which should have priority?

"No nation is anywhere near to practising sustainable development… what is required is a seismic shift in thinking, deriving from a similarly profound shift in perception, on the part of citizens of every sort and condition… from political leaders and policy makers to business chiefs and household heads."

(Norman Myers, *Sustainable Development – Key Concepts,* 1993)

"If Ibsen's 'Enemy of the People' were alive today, he would recognise the ethic that has informed capitalist and communist countries alike – economic growth before public health and well-being. The true enemies of the people are those who continue to sacrifice our long term interests for short term gains. But perhaps we should all look in the mirror."

(Susannah York, *Save the Earth,* 1991)

"So there's a challenge. Ten years to clean up our habits and persuade the corporate giants to release us from industrial slavery. Ten years to persuade hungry moguls to love life more than profit. Ten years to restructure our economic ideas on how the precious harvests of this brow-beaten planet are to be used, and ten years to reassess our priorities in order that Mother Earth can catch her breath before we lose ours. Seems pretty hopeful to me. No problem."

(Ralph Steadman, *Save the Earth,* 1991)

● What is the role of Agenda 21 in all this?
  – All these projects were underway before it was heard of, though some participants believe that they can use it as a lever to get commitment to their ideas from local and central Government.

The beginnings of answers to some of these questions can be found in the case studies, but they are all issues which will require open acknowledgement and discussion if the transition to sustainability is to stand a chance of success.

Ways to use the case studies with groups

Community groups embarking on their own projects, and secondary school or college groups exploring sustainable development, may like to use the case studies or the synopses as a stimulus for discussion.

Activity 1

Ask small groups to read different case studies and to note down key issues or questions arising about the nature of sustainable development and factors that can help it to work in practice.

● Does each case study address sustainable development? If so, how?

● What were the key issues or questions that were raised for each group?

● Were some of them the same for the different case studies?

● Is the whole group able to come up with a common set of issues or questions that illuminate important factors in the process of achieving sustainable development?

Activity 2

Groups can analyse their case studies according to the criteria suggested by Ken Webster (see Introduction, pp10–11, 'How do we measure sustainable development'):

1 The degree to which resource use is linear or cyclical

Are materials or energy being used so that waste is minimised by reuse, recycling or the use of renewable sources?

2 The degree to which human interaction is fragmentary or convivial

Do people meet in the course of their daily lives in a way which encourages them to undertake joint tasks or offer mutual support?

3 The extent to which production and consumption are international, national or local

Are the goods and services people use coming from within their own resources or local area? If so, the need for energy, materials, packaging and transportation will tend to be decreased. (Webster points out that this does not apply to information technology – telephone, video, electronics, etc.)

4 The degree to which the control of an activity is outside the control of local people or is exercised democratically by them

The more people control or influence the production of energy, goods and services, the more they are likely to be able to minimise pollution and environmental damage and ensure equitable costs and rewards.

5 The extent to which an activity diminishes the ecological base or promotes biodiversity

The more an activity reduces or simplifies a habitat, eg through monoculture or by certain fishing techniques, the more likely it is that biodiversity will be decreased. If it adds to the variety of the habitat, biodiversity will increase. Webster suggests that activities which fulfil the first four criteria will tend also to promote biodiversity.

● Which case studies score highest in which areas?

- Does this give us an indication of the kinds of projects which are more likely to achieve sustainability?

Activity 3

Give groups copies of the quotations from the beginning and end of the book – 'Some viewpoints on development' (pp6–7) and 'More thoughts on sustainability' (pp84–85) and ask them to cut them up and rank them in the order that they agree or disagree with them, putting the ones they most agree with at the top and ones they most disagree with at the bottom. They must be prepared to justify their decisions as a group.

Compare rankings between the groups:

- Which statements did most people put near the top?

- Which statements did most people put near the bottom?

- Which statements caused most disagreement?

- Do the quotations reflect different philosophies and priorities?

- Would these philosophies and priorities lead to different preferred solutions?

If the group has already read the case studies, they could discuss which of the philosophies suggested by the quotations are most nearly reflected in the different projects.

International, national or local policies known to the group could also be analysed in terms of which of the philosophies they reflect.

Activity 4

Give groups the following set of questions to work on:

- Could the positive elements from each case study be combined?

- What would the resulting society look like?

- Does this give any insight into the direction societies should be taking to achieve more sustainable ways of living?

- Would the group like to live in such a society or are there parts of their current life styles that they would miss?

- Would a society combining all these elements be fully sustainable, or would there still be areas of life that were unsustainable in the long term?

Activity 5

Select one case study that is relevant to the group. Ask everyone to study the 'downside' section.

Ask for volunteers to play the various individuals and organisations involved in the decision making, and role play a discussion between them which attempts to resolve the problems. Other members of the group can interrupt at any time with suggestions about different lines of argument participants could employ, which could then be played through to find their likely outcome.

At the end, draw together conclusions about what would need to change for there to be a successful resolution of the problems. Who would be able to influence these changes?

The following example suggests some of the characters and viewpoints that could be role played for the Anglian Woodland Project. The arguments could be developed further by the use of additional information from the case study.

ROLE 1 – WOODLAND PROJECT WORKER
You are employed by the project and as well as enjoying your job, you value trees and woodlands for their contribution to the beauty of an area and for their significance as a habitat for plants and animals. You are aware that they have a value greater than can be accounted for economically. You are concerned that ancient

woodlands are being destroyed throughout the world and particularly in East Anglia. Your commitment is to conserving existing woodlands more than to planting new ones because of the length of time it takes eco-systems to develop, particularly on land that has been over-treated with fertilisers, herbicides and pesticides. You believe that non-intervention is not an option, as neglected woodlands will not regenerate naturally.

You believe that greater use of British hardwoods will ensure the future of broadleaved woodlands and limit pollution caused by international transportation and by chemical treatment of softwoods. You are aware that East Anglia is suffering from lack of local employment and believe that managing small woodlands could provide a range of skilled work. You recognise that woodland management will never make a lot of money for the landowners, but believe that most of them would be prepared to do it if it didn't cost them money and you set up the mechanisms to make it happen. The preliminary stages require public finance but you believe that the market for woodland products exists and that long term, the systems could become self-supporting. You believe that industries will invest once they are sure that the resources will be reliably provided long term.

Your interest is in conserving the woodlands but you are not necessarily against their management for pheasant shooting because, done properly, it requires the same process, though you are against short term leasing of land for shooting because it does not encourage long term management . You are most concerned about maintaining biodiversity of species rather than preserving individual plants and animals, and this may mean shooting deer and squirrels and removing invasive plant species or thinning trees to allow for regeneration.

ROLE 2 – LANDOWNER
You run a farm that has been in your family for generations, which you now use mainly to grow wheat. The Common Agricultural Policy subsidies for grain production ensure that you make a reasonable living from it. Over recent years, in response to overproduction of grain, the Government have introduced a policy requiring farmers to set-aside land, but you have found that with greater use of fertilisers, you can continue to grow almost as much grain on less land and thus keep up profits. The only woodland

you have on your farm has been left because it is in small pockets of uneven land, often next to streams, that it would not be possible to plough. Your friends enjoy shooting pheasants there in the season, so you gain some pleasure and income from it too.

You are not particularly interested in doing anything with the woodland, as it seems all right as it is and you don't really have the time to manage it, but people from the Woodland Project have recently suggested to you that if you allowed coppicers onto the land, they would improve the woods. They say it would not cost you anything because the coppicers would use the wood, though you are not convinced that there would be a market for it. You wouldn't mind this as long as it didn't cost you anything but you are a bit concerned that it might affect the pheasants or that the machinery might damage the land. They suggest that you could use wood from your own trees for fencing and hurdles on the farm, though someone would have to make them and it is not expensive to buy such things ready made. They would like you to allow public rights of way through the woods but you don't really want people traipsing across your land as you already have problems of vandalism.

ROLE 3 – RETAILER

You are a national company, selling a large range of goods, including shelving, garden furnishings and barbecue charcoal. You would be happy to be 'environmentally friendly' as long as it didn't affect your profits and lose you shareholders. You buy your wood from large plantations growing mainly conifers, managed to produce quick supplies of straight, knot-free wood . You market this as 'from sustainable forests' because new trees are planted to replace those cut down. It has been suggested to you that the wood does not need to be knot free unless it is for a load-bearing wall, which would mean less wastage, but you believe the customers want wood that looks nice and unmarked.

The British Charcoal Group wanted to supply local charcoal direct to your stores but you have always believed in economies of scale and have bought in bulk, supplying your outlets from a central warehouse. Anyway, as imported charcoal is slightly cheaper, you can't see much point in changing to British. You believe your duty is to supply the customer with what they want as cheaply as possible.

ROLE 4 – GOVERNMENT

You have a complex job to do. You made a promise at the Earth Summit at Rio to try to minimise environmental damage but if it costs taxpayers money they may vote against you at the next election. You would be very happy for there to be more jobs in East Anglia but believe that it is up to private industry to invest in setting up businesses and that they will do so if they think there is a profit to be made. They would also pay taxes on their profits which would enable you to do things which are popular with the public, such as planting new community forests.

At the moment the economy is in a bad way and spending public money on an organisation which employs people to persuade farmers to manage their woodlands is not a priority. You consider that the farmers' job is to provide the country with food and that if they aren't using their woodlands already, it can't be financially viable. You don't feel that you should encourage the use of British wood as manufacturers should have freedom of choice to do what is best for their business and imported wood is often cheaper.

ROLE 5 – PRESERVATIONIST

You have lived in the area all your life and love the small areas of woodland that remain. You believe their preservation is of the utmost importance and that the survival of the planet should come before human need for resources and the desire to make money. Trees are being cut down at a horrific rate all over the world and you believe that we should stop cutting them down in this country. You think that people can do without charcoal for their barbecues and use something else for their fences and furniture and that essential wood can come from forestry plantations. Ancient woodlands have been there for hundreds, sometimes thousands of years and should not be interfered with. You believe public money should be going into planting trees, not cutting them down, for whatever purpose.

You believe all creatures have a right to life and are horrified that some people who say they care about nature will encourage the shooting of an animal as beautiful as a deer. You do not think that we should encourage more people to use the woodlands as that will further disturb the wildlife that lives there.

Activity 6

Focus on a project that the group are working on and draw out from the case studies any lessons that may be relevant to the success of their project.

Draw up a plan of action that takes these lessons into account.

Addresses for further information

Walter Segal Self Build Trust
Unit 213
16 Baldwins Gardens
London EC1N 7RJ
Tel: 0171 831 5696

LETSLINK UK
61, Woodcock Road
Warminster
Wiltshire
BA12 9DH
Tel: 01985 217 871

The Camphill Village Trust
Delrow House
Hilfield Lane
Aldenham
Watford
WD2 8DJ

Iris Water and Design
Langburn Bank
Castleton
Whitby
YO21 2EU
Tel: 01287 660002

Anglian Wooodland Project
Forest Office
Santon Downham
Brandon
Suffolk
IP27 0TJ
Tel: 01842 815826

Birkenhead Central
Neighbourhood College
22 St Anne's Street
Birkenhead
Wirral
L41 3JU

Acknowledgements

The author would like to thank the following people who gave generously of their time, ideas, inspiration and hospitality:

Mike Daligan, Chair, Walter Segal Self Build Trust

Gabrielle Sanders, The Diggers

Steve Cole, Tommy Slattery, Alison and Gerard, SeaSaw

Liz Shepherd, Trace Senior, Harry Turner, Warminster Local Exchange Trading System

Peter Smith, Chris and Val, and the other residents and co-workers of Larchfield Community

Chris Hudson, Iris Water

Bob Hands, Director, Anglian Woodalnd Project

Pete Fordham, Warden and Cathy Harmer, Assistant Warden, Bradfield Woods National Nature Reserve

Val Machin and Jeff Thompson, Project Managers, City Lands

Maureen Corish, Community Action Network Representative, City Lands and Trustee of Wallasey Neighbourhood Resource Centre

Claire Vickers, Manager and Paul Mc Govern, Neighbourhood Worker, Central Birkenhead Neighbourhood College

Phil Champain, WWF-UK

About WWF-UK

WWF (World Wide Fund For Nature) is the world's largest independent environmental organisation, with a global network active in 96 countries.

WWF aims to conserve nature and ecological processes for the benefit of all life on Earth. By stopping, and eventually reversing the degredation of our natural environment, we strive for a future in which people and nature can live in balance.

This mission can only be achieved if people recognise and accept the need for sustainable, just and careful use of natural resources. WWF-UK believes that education has a key role to play in this process. We are therefore working with schools, colleges, further and higher education, with community groups, and with business and industry. Our comprehensive environmental education programme includes resource development, IT projects, curriculum development, professional and vocational training, business toolkits and work with local authorities.

If you would like further details about WWF-UK's education programme, please write to:
WWF-UK, Education and Awareness, Panda House, Weyside Park, Godalming, Surrey GU7 1XR.
Telephone: 01483 426444.
Fax: 01483 426409.
Web site address: http://www.wwf-uk.org